"There are those who would ask, 'What has New York to do with Jerusalem or the arts with religion?' Steve Turner answers that question as he calls the believing aesthete and the Christian church to come to the table, sit down and talk. In this informed and rare treatment, Turner challenges the Christian community to encourage the artist's voice to be heard and then challenges believing artists to allow their art to be influenced and enhanced by sound theology."

JIM THOMAS, MUSICIAN & AUTHOR

"*Imagine* is a wake-up call to the Christian community to fulfill the cultural mandate and to develop a theology of creativity that both embraces our humanness and engages the world with 'muscular' Christianity. Author Steve Turner addresses the church and its involvement in the arts with a prophetic challenge, an appeal to be salt and light in our world instead of withdrawing into mere Christian subculture or pietistic retreat. But he is eminently balanced in his challenge to those of us who have accepted a call to be 'in the world' of arts/entertainment but not of it. He helps us break out of the compartmentalization and secular-sacred dichotomy that so often paralyzes the Christian artist and community from real impact on our world.

"As a screenwriter in Hollywood, my heart was exhorted with his warning of those who have gradually shipwrecked their faith through incremental assimilation of the very world they are trying to reach. With a strong and decisive commitment to Christ, Scripture and truth, he helps draw guidelines for avoiding the ignorance of all extremes when approaching the arts.

"If you are a Christian who consumes culture without discrimination, then you need to read this book. If you are a Christian who considers arts and entertainment to be worldly or a waste of time, then you need to read this book. And if you are a Christian who thinks you want to serve the Lord by being a light in the darkness of any creative industry today, you need to read this book."

BRIAN GODAWA, SCREENWRITER, *TO END ALL WARS*

"I have long been a fan of Steve Turner's poetry and journalism—he has a way of illuminating the intersection of the sacred and the secular in our lives. Now, in *Imagine* he lets us glimpse behind the curtain and see the philosophy that undergirds his work. Highly readable, insightful and provocative, *Imagine* draws on historical and contemporary examples and biblical insights to offer a refreshing and balanced perspective on how faith can inform our creativity. Turner challenges us to move beyond our ghetto mentality and engage our culture with art that is creative, authentic and relevant. His book should be required reading for every Christian interested in the arts."

TERRY GLASPEY, AUTHOR, *BOOK LOVER'S GUIDE TO GREAT READING* & *NOT A TAME LION: THE SPIRITUAL LEGACY OF C. S. LEWIS*

imagine.

a vision for
christians
in the
arts

steve
turner

IVP Books

An imprint of InterVarsity Press
Downers Grove, Illinois

InterVarsity Press
P.O. Box 1400, Downers Grove, IL 60515-1426
World Wide Web: www.ivpress.com
E-mail: email@ivpress.com

InterVarsity Press® is the book-publishing division of InterVarsity Christian Fellowship/USA®, a student movement active on campus at hundreds of universities, colleges and schools of nursing in the United States of America, and a member movement of the International Fellowship of Evangelical Students. For information about local and regional activities, write Public Relations Dept., InterVarsity Christian Fellowship/USA, 6400 Schroeder Rd., P.O. Box 7895, Madison, WI 53707-7895, or visit the IVCF website at <www.intervarsity.org>.

Cover illustration: Gil Mayers/Superstock

ISBN-10: 0-8308-2291-7
ISBN-13: 978-0-8308-2291-1

Printed in the United States of America ∞

Library of Congress Cataloging-in-Publication Data

Turner, Steve, 1949-
  Imagine : a vision for Christians in the arts / Steve Turner.
    p. cm.
  Includes bibliographical references.
  ISBN 0-8308-2291-7 (pbk. : alk. paper)
  1. Christianity and the arts. I. Title.
 BR115.A8 T87 2001
 261.5'7—dc21

2001016775

P	23	22	21	20	19	18	17	16	15	14	13	12	11	10
Y	21	20	19	18	17	16	15	14	13	12	11	10	09	

To Nigel Goodwin, who rescued me, and
to my wife, Mo, who keeps me going.

"How shall we sing the Lord's song in a strange land?"

PSALM 137:4 *(KJV)*

contents

Introduction

The origins of this book grew out of a lecture I gave to two groups of musicians in Nashville and Los Angeles in 1998. Steve Taylor, recording artist and producer of Sixpence None The Richer, in whose home the Nashville meeting took place, then published the text of the talk through his multimedia company Squint under the title of "Being There: A Vision for Christianity and the Arts."

The response to the lecture and the booklet convinced me to consider expanding the argument into a book. I wasn't kidding myself that I had something original to say, but I knew that there were a lot of people out there who still needed to hear that it was possible to integrate their faith with their art.

At one of the meetings a young musician came up to me and explained that his father, a pastor, thought he should be using his music for the glory of God and that if he didn't use it for the glory of God, he was sinning. He wanted to know what I thought he should do.

Where do you begin? I don't doubt that the father was a sincere believer genuinely concerned that his son live his life in the right way. I also don't doubt that the son was a sincere believer concerned to live his life in the right way. The problem comes because the word *glory* comes with cultural overtones. Some people think you are only really glorifying God if you are doing something religious.

Over the years I have met many artists who have found themselves in a dilemma similar to that of the young musician. They want to "serve God," but they don't particularly want to be confined to a narrow religious market. They want to create something that reflects the passions and concerns of their faith, but they want to compete alongside their nonbelieving contemporaries. On the one hand, they are usually frustrated that there is so little distinctive Christian content in the contemporary arts, but on the other hand, they are embarrassed at the low standards of much of what is promoted as "Christian art."

Whenever I meet someone like this I'm able to share experiences from my own career as a poet (for both adults and children), biographer, travel writer, journalist and rock music critic. Over the years I have been fortunate to meet Christians from around the world working as artists who share the same vision. I have learned a lot from them.

What I can say when I meet an individual is limited. This book is really what I would say to them if I had a few days to talk. It begins autobiographically to emphasize the fact that I am writing not as an academic but as someone who has had to do his learning on the job. I have great respect for academic theses on the subject, but in my experience they often fail to reach the people who are making the art.

I may have been a little ambitious in addressing the arts in general rather than one art form in particular, but I thought there were advantages in highlighting principles that could be applied to all disciplines. I tried to bear all the arts in mind all the time, but there is an obvious bias toward literature and music simply because they are the arts I know best. I have tried to have a broad understanding of the arts, which means including such popular arts as rock music and cinema alongside the longer established arts of theater and painting. I have also been generous in my use of the word *Christian* to describe artists. I realize that only God knows who are his, but if someone claims to be a Christian, their work evidences the view commonly held by Christians, and there is no glaring inconsistency in their public lives, for the purposes of the following discussion I have been happy to call them Christian.

The important people in the genesis of this project have been Mark Joseph, who brought me to America to deliver the original lecture, Steve Taylor, who saw the potential of turning it into a book, Andy Le Peau of IVP, who commissioned the book, and Howard and Roberta Ahmanson of Fieldstead and Company, who graciously funded my research and writing time.

one

the vision

In 1970 I was a student at L'Abri, a small learning community founded by Dr. Francis Schaeffer in the mountains of Switzerland, where people came from around the world to try to make sense of their lives and times in the light of Christian truth.

Life at L'Abri sharpened our perceptions. Many of us had come from backgrounds which encouraged us to categorize all culture as either Christian or non-Christian, spiritual or fleshly. Schaeffer, influenced by the Dutch art historian Hans Rookmaaker, instead proposed that we should look at works individually. Rather than asking, Is this artist saved? ask, Is this piece of work technically excellent? Is it a valid expression of the artist's view of the world? Are form and content well integrated? Is truth communicated?

The effect was liberating. Using the old categories, the Beatles, who dominated pop culture at the time, were definitely of the world, the flesh and the devil. None of them professed to be Christian, their songs didn't openly glorify God, and they took illegal drugs. However, looking at their art in this new way, different considerations predominated. Did they display technical excellence? Was their work a valid expression of the way they saw things? Did what they have to say integrate with the way in which they chose to say it? Was any truth communicated in the songs?

Evangelical Christians traditionally had taken redemption as their starting point to anything. Had the artist been reborn and was the artist singing, writing or painting about being reborn? For Schaeffer, creation was the starting point. Everyone was made in God's image and those blessed with artistic gifts couldn't help but display that original image in some way.

This perspective confirmed what I had instinctively felt for some time—that a lot of art created by Christians was bad and a lot of art created by non-Christians was good. It was possible for a well-loved hymn to be bad art and a painting by an utter reprobate to be good art. By making truth the sole criterion, Christians had often diminished the importance of human endeavor in the arts, and in doing this had deprived themselves of a wealth of cultural experience.

Then again, the truth that most concerned them was only part of the whole truth anyway. The complexities of human life were overlooked in a search for "the simple truth." Christian fiction, for example, lacked the deep texture of real life because its writers were merely using the form to evangelize people whom they imagined would be adverse to the gospel in any other form.

The lack of Christians in the popular arts and the inferior quality of contemporary "Christian art" had an effect on me as a teenager. Because its claims were ignored, Christianity appeared to be culturally irrelevant. Did this mean that Christians just couldn't tough it out in the "real" world? Did it mean that cultural expressions of Christianity could only survive when unchallenged, in the cordoned off enclave of the Christian subculture?

Because the work that bore the name Christian was often poor in quality and naive in understanding, Christianity by implication seemed insipid and uninspiring. How great was this God who allowed such work to represent him? How exciting was this life that seemed to prefer drabness to color, shallowness to complexity, security to risk?

My experience at L'Abri convinced me that Christians not only *could* be active in the popular arts, they *should* be. This was crystallized for me when someone arrived at L'Abri from America with a copy of *Déjà Vu*, the latest album from Crosby, Stills, Nash and Young. A group of us sat as the album was played, our ears keenly attuned to the lyrics, listening for any nuance that would suggest where our generation was headed.

This was an age when rock music was the lightning rod of cultural change. The words of people like Bob Dylan, Jim Morrison, Paul Simon, Jerry Garcia, Pete Townshend, John Lennon and Paul McCartney were scrutinized for wisdom. Musicians were no longer simply entertainers but prophets and shamans. Timothy Leary, a former professor of psychology at Harvard who had become a proselytizer for the spiritual benefits of LSD, said that rock 'n' roll musicians were "the philosopher-poets of the new religion."[1]

This reverence may have been unmerited, but rock music was responding to the upheavals of the 1960s more instantly than any other art form. The Beatles recorded "All You Need Is Love" while American troops fought in Vietnam and young people marched for peace. The antiwar protests in London during the summer of 1968 inspired "Street Fighting Man" by the Rolling Stones. The shootings at Kent State University in August 1970 led Neil Young to write "Ohio" as the news broke and it was released as a CSNY single eight days later.

The final track on the first side of *Déjà Vu* was the song "Woodstock." Written by Joni Mitchell in response to the huge rock festival that had taken place the previous summer ("Three days of love, peace and music," as the documentary film of the event was later advertised), the song represented the high point of the 1960s dream of an alternative society. Believers in a counterculture thought it exemplified a new commitment to basic human values and a rejection of greed, war, hypocrisy and exploitation.

Mitchell captured this essentially religious vision. In the song she meets a boy ("a child of God") on his way to the festival and asks him what he's doing. The boy answers that he's going to get back to the land to "set my soul free"—and then comes the chorus, as if sung by everyone at the festival who shared the same hope:

> We are stardust
> We are golden
> We are billion year old carbon
> And we've got to get ourselves
> Back to the garden.

The last two lines struck me. Here was a rock supergroup alluding to the Garden of Eden. The rest of the song made clear that this wasn't a call for Christian conversion, but it was at least an admission that humans were in need of spiritual renewal. Where were the Christians who were anything like their equals in the business who could have engaged with this profound metaphor? Most of the Christian musicians I knew of were involved in "Christian music," which at that time meant playing Scripture-inspired songs to gatherings of believers. Even the sharpest song by these practitioners would not have an impact on the debate because it wouldn't be heard by the key debaters.

"Woodstock" expressed a conviction that we were created to be great ("stardust," "golden") but that something had gone wrong (caught in "the devil's bargain") and that we needed to return to an original innocence ("back to the garden"). In this recreated world the instruments of oppression and violence would be changed into objects of beauty. Bombers would turn into butterflies, just as the Old Testament prophets foresaw a time when swords would be turned into plowshares and spears into pruning hooks.

The difference between believers and unbelievers in this respect was often not in the issues that engaged them but in the conclusions reached. We might agree that humans have dignity yet disagree over the source of that dignity. We might agree that humans have been separated from their original destiny but disagree over how and when that took place. We might agree that humans need to be transformed but disagree over how that can be achieved.

Looked at with the benefit of thirty years of hindsight, "Woodstock" appears naive. The idealism of five hundred thousand young people at an American music festival didn't signal a huge change in the behavior of the species. The problems, such as violence and pollution, remain and may even be worse. The song implies a belief in the evolution of human nature ("maybe it's the time of man"), and this unfounded optimism is its ultimate weakness.

Yet "Woodstock" was an attempt, within popular culture, to raise some of the most important questions that humans ever ask. Who are we? What makes us significant? What has gone wrong? How can we be restored? I wanted Christians to contribute to this debate. Aware of the issues being discussed, I found it puzzling that we weren't already there. Wasn't this the very stuff that we were so good at talking about?

Actually, if I'm honest, I didn't find it surprising, because I grew up in the evangelicalism that didn't prepare people for a dynamic role in secular culture. I could understand why the best-known Christian movie actor of the time was the cowboy entertainer Roy Rogers and why there was no best-known rock singer or painter. What I did find was that this situation no longer made sense.

No one ever told me that it would be wrong for a Christian to become an actor or a songwriter, a novelist or a dancer. It was implied. There were no role models. I can remember a well-known actress and a British pop singer getting saved, but then they gave up their careers "for the Lord." Their testimony was obviously more highly valued than their talent. Like drunkenness and promiscuity, involvement in the arts was something best spoken of in the past tense.

Christians seemed to acknowledge a work hierarchy. Evangelists and those in "full-time ministry" were at the top. Doctors, nurses and people in the caring professions came next. Then there were teachers, policemen and the great mass of workers. Artists, media representatives and people in show business would have been in the lowest possible group if they had been mentioned at all.

Consistently, Christians didn't consume much art either. On the whole they didn't own televisions ("the devil's box"), collect art or go to the theater. Fiction, like dancing, was okay for children but not for adults. Rock music was worldly. Movies were suitable only if they were cartoons, family entertainment or, oddly enough, fact-based war epics. The reasoning was that most art was created by nonbelievers and could therefore damage our spiritual health. We sang a chorus that ran:

Be careful little eyes what you see
Be careful little eyes what you see
For there's a God up above
Who is looking down in love
So be careful little eyes what you see.

Not knowing what God's tastes were but expecting him to be a bit prudish, it seemed best to play safe. Additionally, art was considered a waste of time. All we needed to know about life was in the Bible. Anything else was superfluous. What could these spiritually dead people teach us that we didn't already know?

To be entertained suggested that our minds were being taken off things for a while, and Christians weren't supposed to have their minds taken off things. Anything that distracted us from Bible reading, prayer and witnessing slowed down the process of sanctification. Evangelical churches were sparsely decorated because it was thought that simplicity focused devotion, and God had little concern for outward appearances. Garrison Keillor accurately captures this attitude in his novel *Lake Wobegon Days* when he describes a typical meeting of the Sanctified Brethren, "a sect so tiny that that nobody but us and God knew about it." The group met every Sunday in a living room with plain folding chairs: "No clergyman in a black smock. No organ or piano, for that would make one person too prominent. No upholstery, it would lead to complacency. No picture of Jesus, He was in our hearts. . . . No musical notation, for music must come from the heart and not off a page."[2]

When Christians did on rare occasions employ the arts it was as "outreach." The arts, we were told, could be "used." They could be "effective tools for evangelism." Thus we had movies with tissue thin characters and threadbare plots that moved inexorably toward climactic conversions. We had singer-songwriters with a beat to capture the attention and a "message" to be given in the lyric. We even had Christian novels that coated the gospel in the candy of fiction.

When I said that I would like to be a writer, an older Christian said to me, "That would be nice. There are some good Christian magazines around," the assumption being that Christians should write for Christians about Christianity. The idea that I might want to write for a national newspaper or magazine on general issues wasn't considered.

Instinctively I felt that this was not right. I didn't yet have the theology to back it up, just a gut feeling that Christians could, and should, be involved in all areas of culture. I soon met others with similar instincts. I read a report in a Christian newspaper about an actor, Nigel Goodwin, who was referring to contemporary poets, media guru Marshall McLuhan and the Beatles in his lectures. I was not only surprised that a Christian speaker knew of McLuhan or could quote from contemporary poetry but that he was using their work in a defense of the faith.

Nigel was a man full of life and love for God, who was also a great fan of popular culture. On our first meeting he excitedly showed me a book called *Rock and Other Four Letter Words* by J. Marks,[3] Calvin Tomkins' study of the avant-garde, *Ahead of the Game*,[4] and John Russell Taylor's *Anger and After*,[5] which looked at British theater since John Osborne. I was impressed with this believer who not only wasn't threatened by the secular arts but obviously delighted in them.

He then asked me if I had ever heard of Francis Schaeffer. I hadn't, and he handed me the then recently published *The God Who Is There*,[6] a survey of trends in art, philosophy and religion. As I flipped through its pages the names of Jung, Cage, Picasso and Dylan Thomas jumped out at me. Maybe I had led a sheltered life, but I had never seen the works of such artists used as part of a Christian apologetic.

It proved to be an important turning point for me. Within a year I was in Switzerland studying at L'Abri. Schaeffer and his associates shared a passion for culture both as consumers and as critics. They approached the work of artists with sensitivity and respect. As they analyzed worldviews and measured them against biblical truth, it increased my conviction that Christians should be contributing to the dialogue.

The most powerful message emanating from L'Abri was "Jesus is Lord." That meant that the risen Christ was Lord of mealtimes and storytelling, banking and business, art and culture. There was no area of life about which we could say to him—"I'm sorry. You better keep out of this. You wouldn't understand. Stick to religion."

While I was there I questioned the young American travelers I met about the latest hip books and through their tips began reading the short stories of Richard Brautigan, the journalism of Tom Wolfe and the fiction of Richard Farina. I envisaged a literature that would have a cool "pop" surface but would deal with the profound issues that preoccupied us at L'Abri. My newfound buddy, Mark Quinn, and I decided that we'd write a novel together. It was going to be called *Ripped-Off Kids*, but our bank of ideas began and ended with the title.

Although I had no literary credentials I was determined to go to London and become a writer after leaving L'Abri. Three months later I was living in North London, packing books in a warehouse by day and working as a freelance journalist for a rock magazine by night. During a short period I interviewed three important British rock acts—Jethro Tull, Marc Bolan of T. Rex and Rod Stewart—and then, liking what I had submitted, the magazine offered me a job. I became a full-time writer.

Over the next few years I found myself interviewing some of the best-known musicians of the period, including Elton John, Lou Reed, Frank Zappa, Eric Clapton and David Bowie, and members of The Who, Rolling Stones, The Band, The Moody Blues, The Byrds, Pink Floyd, Queen and Grateful Dead. I even found myself in Los Angeles sharing my poetry and discussing hippie idealism with David Crosby and Graham Nash, whose version of "Woodstock" had played a part in my journey.

I had to determine the responsibilities of a Christian journalist working on a magazine for the general market. I was being hired to convey information about music and musicians to a readership. I would have been failing my employer if I had neglected to do this in favor of expounding theology.

However, every article, if written with consideration and integrity, would show my view of the world through direct opinion, choice of subject matter or the priority given to information. As an interviewer my questions would be different, and I would therefore elicit different responses. I would challenge views that might otherwise have gone unchallenged.

I felt that I was beginning to fulfill the vision I had been given at L'Abri. The magazine I worked for didn't have the impact of *Time* or even *Rolling Stone*, but it gave me journalistic experience and access to significant creative figures. Above all, it meant that I could play a small part in the cultural debate.

As a journalist my job was to get a story rather than to evangelize, but just like any other Christian, I needed to be ready to discuss spiritual matters if they were raised. I would pray for the direction of each interview and the confidence to speak up if necessary. I didn't want to be where it counted and yet be silent about the things that mattered most to me.

When I interviewed John Lennon at the time of his album *Imagine*, he suddenly flipped open a newspaper that had been sent to him by members of one of the new Jesus people communities that were springing up in America as evangelicalism began meeting the needs of the hippie generation. The centerfold was an open letter to the former Beatle written by a fan who had become a Christian. The essential message was "You need Jesus, John."

Lennon read the whole letter to me, put the paper down on his desk and asked, "What do you think of that?" I'm sure he was expecting me to pour scorn on the correspondent, as most other music journalists would have done, but I didn't. Instead we had a debate about the nature of Christianity ("I know all that Christian jazz") in which he listened to me explain my faith ("Well, good luck to you") and gave me a few of his own ideas ("God is a concept by which we measure our pain").

Being a journalist allowed me to observe the creative process at close quarters. Bands would ask my opinion of demo tapes, producers would show me how certain studio effects were created, songwriters would share material that they had only just written. (I wish I'd kept the interview tape where David Bowie previewed his new song "Andy Warhol" for me while I paid a visit to the bathroom.)

All the time I was reporting on these rock musicians I was writing and performing my own poetry. I was happy to contribute to Christian events but saw my main calling as being in the coffee bars and folk clubs where the new oral poetry scene was taking off. I resented ever being described as a "Christian poet" because the label was too confining. I believed that Christians should be writing poetry infused with godly perception rather than poetry about religion.

My thinking of these matters was helped by three books in particular: *The Christian Mind* by Harry Blamires,[7] *Selected Essays* by T. S. Eliot[8] and *The Gospel According to Peanuts* by Robert Short.[9] Blamires argued forcefully that there was a need to "think Christianly" on all subjects and not to confine our religious thinking to religion. Eliot, in his essay "Religion and Literature," called for a literature that would be "unconsciously, rather than deliberately and defiantly Christian." Short took the Peanuts cartoon strips of Charles Schulz and showed how they explored gospel values through humor.

My first collection of poems, *Tonight We Will Fake Love*, was published in London in 1975 by the book division of a record company which had announced that it was looking for literary equivalents to the Beatles and Neil Young. *The Daily Mail*, a British newspaper, reviewed it under the headline, "At last, a poet with all the flair of a rock number." Significantly, for me, the writer identified what he called a "Christian twist" in the poems.

The arts remain an important forum for debate in our culture. Although it is not the primary concern of all artists to make statements about the human condition or to create a commentary on the times, it is inevitable that many will do so simply because the instinct of the artist is to ask questions about origins, identity, behavior and destiny. The jazz musician Max Roach once said, "Two theories (of art) exist. One is that art is for the sake of art. That is true. The other theory, which is also true, is that the artist is like a secretary. . . . He keeps a record of his time. My music tries to say how I really feel, and I hope it mirrors in some way how black people feel in the United States."[10]

As I will explain in more detail later in the book, I don't believe every artist who is a Christian should produce art that is a paraphrased sermon. A lot of Christian art is for the sake of art. But because art is also a record and reflects the questions and anxieties of the time, I would like to see contributions that reflect a Christian understanding of that time. I also would like to see them in the mainstream arts rather than in the religious subculture.

I am not saying this for evangelistic reasons. I don't expect art to convert people, although I realize that art plays an important part in shaping our understanding of the world. I am saying it because debates are taking place in cinema, painting, dance, fiction, poetry and theater on issues where Christians have something to give, and yet they are not even being heard.

I think we should be in those debates as part of our mandate to look after and care for the world rather than because of the command to make disciples. We are not entering the debates to tell people what to believe. Art tends to show rather than to tell. It allows people the opportunity to experience another way of seeing the world. But if we are not there, people are denied the opportunity of encountering our perspective.

The Christian artist will often be an irritant, disturbing the anthropocentric view of the world that fallen nature naturally gravitates toward. Just as people think they have removed God from all consideration of a particular question, the Christian annoyingly puts him back on the agenda in some way. And when God is back on the agenda, people are forced to deal with him, even if only to try to marginalize him again.

A Christian understanding is still absent both in commercial art and in the experimental fringes. It's rare to find Christians directing in Hollywood, producing serious fiction or writing plays for London's West End or New York's Broadway. It's even more rare to find them in the alternative arts venues, comedy clubs and contemporary dance theaters. The average young cultured person would be hard-pressed to name a single contemporary Christian screenwriter, dramatist, choreographer, novelist, comedian or painter, even though Christianity remains the dominant religion in both Europe and the Americas. When *Time* magazine compiled a list of the one hundred most significant people in twentieth-century art and entertainment there were only five who had shown any public signs of Christian faith.

The aim of this book is to explore the reasons why things are this way in the hope that, through understanding, changes may take place and that Christians who are artists will feel valued, encouraged, inspired and emboldened.

two

the church

O*ne of the great hindrances to the development of biblically* informed mainstream art has been the perception that Christians should make "Christian art" and that "Christian art" is always explicitly religious. Understood in this way, "Christian art" is not distinguished by a regenerated outlook on the whole of life but by a narrow focus on Bible stories, saints, martyrs and the individual's relationship with God.

"Christian art," in this sense, is usually either an aid to worship or a means of evangelism. Not surprisingly, it developed and flourished at a time when Christianity offered the commonly accepted explanation for life. When Dante wrote *The Divine Comedy* and Michelangelo painted *The Last Judgment*, their assumptions about God and Satan, heaven and hell, death and judgment were uncontroversial. They lived in an age when, for most people, there was no alternative explanation of how we came to be here, how we should behave and what happens to us when we die.

From the time of Constantine to the Enlightenment, Christian ideas dominated art for the simple reason that the church had a powerful grasp over every aspect of life. There may well have been as many unregenerate people then as now, but they were unregenerate people who nevertheless understood their lives in terms of creation, fall and redemption. Painters routinely tackled subjects such as the Madonna and child, the crucifixion and the torments of hell.

Yet for the first two centuries after the death and resurrection of Christ, at a point when Christians were a ridiculed minority, the church made no religious art that we know of. Places of worship were not distinguished by paintings, sculptures or special architecture, and Christians had no shrines or venerated images in their homes. If an artist or craftsman converted, they were encouraged to continue with their gift in the everyday world. As late as the fourth century, Eusebius, bishop of Caesarea, could confidently tell Constantine's sister, who had requested a portrait of Christ, that there was no such thing as Christian art.

This wasn't strictly true because for at least a century Christians had been carving symbols (such as fish, doves, palm trees, anchors, shepherds and significant letters of the alphabet) into the walls of the catacombs in Rome and decorating some tombs with illustrations from Old Testament stories. But it was true inasmuch as Christians refrained from portraying God or Christ and didn't emulate the pagans in creating idols. In fact, Christians were so distinguished by their lack of overtly religious art that the pagans derided them. How could this be a real religion capable of stirring worship and devotion if it didn't have any physical representations to bow down before?

This Christian reluctance to make conventional religious art was because of the Old Testament prohibition against making idols "in the form of anything in heaven above or on the earth beneath or in the waters below" (Exodus 20:4). Although the stress of the command was against idol worship, which deprived God of glory that was deservedly his, Christians also deduced an implicit warning to fallen humans never to attempt to portray spirit and holiness. The only image of God necessary in a church was the one in each person.

The departure from this strict interpretation came when Christianity was adopted as the religion of the Roman Empire and took on many of the trappings of imperialism. The power of Rome had been reinforced through images and majestic architecture, and Constantine was keen that the Christian church should follow suit. The once persecuted believers, emboldened with their new status, began to illustrate the walls of churches with scenes from the Bible. Eager to provide a religious experience that didn't disappoint those coming from pagan backgrounds, they allowed domestic shrines and encouraged devotion to images of Mary and the saints.

In this new climate, where "Christian art" was developing, the belief was that visual images helped people worship and communicated truths to the illiterate, but it wasn't long before the line between aids to worship and objects of worship became less distinct. Iconographers created "holy portraits," usually of Christ or a saint, which were meant to be a meeting point between heaven and earth. An icon, according to the contemporary church historian Owen Chadwick, was "something more than a picture on wood. It was seen to have a kinship in spirit with the person painted on it; it could receive the veneration and prayers addressed to the saint, and transmit his or her blessing to the person praying before it. It presented a saint to the soul."[1]

By the eighth century the church itself was becoming uneasy with the role of icons. There were those, known as iconodules, who argued that by becoming a man in Christ, God had established a precedent for giving physical form to divinity. The talent of the artist and the materials used were also gifts of God. The iconoclasts disagreed; they said that it wasn't possible to paint glory, either that of God or that surrounding Mary and the saints.

It took an ecumenical council in 787 to sort out the problem. The eventual decision favored the iconodules but not without reservation. Icons, it was decided, could be used to venerate the person pictured but not to worship them, because only God could be worshiped. The use of statues, however, was banned because, in the eyes of the council, their use had been perverted over the centuries.

As the church grew, new art forms were created, and old art forms were put to Christian use. Bells were used to summon people to worship. Stained-glass windows became known as "the gospel of those who cannot read." Manuscripts were beautifully illuminated by monks. The first hymns were written down, and new forms of music, such as plainsong, were created to take advantage of the unprecedented size of churches and cathedrals. Iconography became one of the issues that contributed to the Great Schism of the eleventh century, when the Eastern church and the Western church separated. Although Catholicism retained the use of representational art, it was in the Orthodox Church that they became central and remain so today.

During the period when the church of Rome was at the center of European power it was the major sponsor of painting and sculpture. Michelangelo's best known work was commissioned directly by various popes, and he was eventually made chief architect of St. Peter's, Rome. Raphael did work for individual churches and cathedrals. Much of Bosch's art was paid for by the Brotherhood of Our Lady, a Christian fraternity of which he was a member.

The church commissioned art that was to be used in places of worship, burial or ecclesiastical business, and so the images it requested were overtly religious. The most popular subjects were, naturally, stories from the Bible, especially the birth, death and resurrection of Christ. Sometimes the relevance of these stories was emphasized by dressing the participants in contemporary clothes. Artists concentrated on capturing the imagined emotions of those who witnessed the incarnation first hand.

Yet great as these works are, they left the impression that "Christian art" should be preoccupied with events described in the Bible. The gap between the everyday experiences of ordinary European believers and these paintings of cherubs, angels and beatific bystanders was every bit as wide as that which existed between their small smoke-filled dwelling places and the huge arches of the then-modern cathedrals.

Ironically it was the Protestant Reformation of the sixteenth century which brought to an end the dominance of this form of "Christian art." Initially the Reformation weakened the authority of Catholicism and reduced its ability to act as the major benefactor for artists. When country gentlemen, nobles, landowners and merchants took over as commissioners of the arts, the subject matter began to change accordingly. These people wanted landscapes, family portraits, paintings of their horses and evocations of foreign cities. They rarely wanted saints and martyrs.

Second, the Protestants were so opposed to the decoration of church buildings that they destroyed "Christian art." Statues, vestments, sacred vessels, mural paintings, stained glass and illuminated manuscripts were ripped, smashed and burned all over Europe. "The Reformation under Edward VI was the worst artistic disaster which ever happened to England," wrote Shakespearean scholar G. B. Harrison. "Moreover, the demand for such works of art suddenly ceased and the traditions of generations of craftsmen were lost."[2]

Third, Protestantism claimed the nonreligious aspects of life for God. If Christ was Lord, he was Lord over all, not simply over our times of prayer, worship and Bible study. In the early sixteenth century, the way of the celibate monk or nun was seen as the ultimate in Christian living. The religious were cut off from all worldly influence, lived in deliberate discomfort and spent almost all of their waking hours in devotional activities. The Reformers challenged this. They argued that even the humblest street sweeper could work to the glory of God.

This liberated the art made by Christians because it allowed art that wasn't explicitly religious yet was soaked in biblical values. One of the most frequently cited examples of this is the work of Rembrandt. We don't have a record of Rembrandt's personal beliefs but know that he was raised in the Reformed Church in Holland, and it is assumed that he would have been taught the Bible from a Calvinist viewpoint when at school.

Although Rembrandt did etchings of biblical scenes, the majority of his paintings were of common people in everyday situations. This was unusual at a time when art focused on religion, classical mythology, and portraiture of the rich and powerful. It appears that his Reformed view of the world was significant in this choice and particularly affected his desire to dignify people and activities previously considered lowly.

This reflected the spirit of the Gospels where Christ gives dignity to the despised—a Bethlehem stable, shepherds, Nazareth, lepers, the blind, Galilean fishermen, Samaritans and the woman at the well. Except for his temple visits and the record of him reading in a synagogue Jesus is never placed in an obviously religious setting.

Rembrandt didn't idealize his subjects. He painted what he saw, which was a mixture of glory and fallenness. He was criticized by his contemporaries for using washerwomen as his models rather than women who looked like Greek goddesses. The Dutch poet Andries Pels (1631-1681) wrote mockingly of these models:

> Flabby breasts,
> Ill-shaped hands, nay, the traces of the lacings.
> Of the corsets on the stomach, of the garters on the legs,
> Must be visible, if Nature was to get her due.[3]

Rembrandt was being, to refer back to Eliot's words, "unconsciously, rather than deliberately and defiantly Christian." Rembrandt was portraying ordinary humans as though through the eyes of Jesus, valuing them for their humanity rather than for their social standing or their wealth. He treats them tenderly yet honestly. He sees the soul beneath the sagging skin.

For the theater, the Reformation had contradictory effects. English drama was revitalized because it made possible debate, dissent and self-expression. The Elizabethan theater was a result of this liberation from enforced orthodoxy. Shakespeare felt free to explore history, behavior and morality without the need to create work that was recognizably religious.

Yet the Puritan authorities hated and feared the theater because it portrayed immorality and could be used to promote subversive ideas. A treatise published in 1616 by a Puritan who signed himself T. G. cited seven reasons why Christians should neither be players nor playgoers: (1) The theater has its origin in pagan ritual. (2) Plays deal in "murder and mischief." (3) The players take on false names, often wear inappropriate clothes and have to act out sins. (4) By approving of plays we take part in the sins they act out. (5) The fruit of playgoing is ill-spent money, time wasted and the New Man is weakened. (6) The church historically has warned its members against the theater. (7) God has judged the theater by allowing accidents to happen to actors and playgoers.

Periodically theaters were closed down when the plays were considered too seditious or bawdy. In 1549 Edward VI banned plays from taking place within the city of London because they "contain matter tending to sedition and contempt for sundry good orders and laws." It was for this reason that the Globe and Rose theaters were built just outside the city, on the south bank of the River Thames. Under the reign of Queen Elizabeth I, players were classified as "vagabonds" if they didn't have homes (and most, because of their travels, did not), and the penalty for being a vagabond, conveniently, was execution.

Disapproval of the theater crops up in the writing of many of the great Christians over the subsequent centuries. Theater was often bracketed with drunkenness, cursing, gambling, card playing and immorality as something worldly in itself. In 1787 the social reformer and evangelical Christian William Wilberforce wrote in a letter to his sister: "I think the tendency of the theater most pernicious."[4] George Müller, the pietist founder of Christian orphanages in England during the nineteenth century, felt the same way. Following his conversion he only went to the theater twice and recalled of the first visit: "I went to a concert but felt that it was unbecoming for me, as a Child of God, to be in such a place."[5]

The Reformation had a similarly ambiguous role in the rise of the novel. On the one hand, scholars generally say the change in thinking brought about by the Reformation made this new genre of literature possible. The teachings of the Puritans and other dissenters focused on the concept of the morally responsible individual and emphasized introspective thinking. In order to analyze their motives, Puritans became great keepers of journals to record spiritual growth and confession of sin. This not only encouraged the act of writing but developed an acute awareness of the inner voice of conscience.

Daniel Defoe's *Robinson Crusoe*[6] is frequently cited as the first significant English novel. Defoe came from a Calvinistic home and was educated at a dissenting academy. Ian Watt, former professor of English at Stanford University, argues that the subjective and individualist spiritual pattern of the early novel was a direct result of such nonconformist Christianity. The novel "outdoes other literary forms in bringing us close to the inward moral being of the individual," Watt writes in *The Rise of the English Novel*. "It achieves this closeness to the inner life of the protagonist by using as a formal basis the autobiographical memoir which was the most immediate and widespread literary expression of the introspective tendency of Puritanism in general."[7]

On the other hand, although nonconformist Christianity had provided the intellectual framework to allow the novel to develop, it didn't approve of fiction. Leisure itself, previously restricted to the upper classes, was a contentious issue now that the lower classes had more of it. The powerful elite worried that they wouldn't use it in a godly way.

Christians were uneasy about unoccupied time ("the devil always finds work for idle hands") and believed that it should be used for self-improvement rather than for amusement. They frowned on activities such as playing cards, which had no goal other than distracting the mind from the worries of the day. Books, they thought, should encourage moral and spiritual development.

But there was an additional reason for avoiding fiction. Novels recounted events that had never actually happened as if they had happened. In other words, in order to enjoy a novel the reader had to believe a lie. Serious-minded Christians didn't see how that could be right.

This attitude is well illustrated by a comment made in 1893 by the Scottish Brethren preacher John Ritchie who was asked the question, "Do you see any objection to a believer reading a high-class work of fiction?" He did: "Novels—the best of them—are lies, and so to speak of high-class falsehood is strange language. . . . Can any child of God be helped in spiritual life by that? Certainly not. Our advice, therefore, is, have nothing whatever to do with fiction. Read and meditate on the Word of God."[8]

Fast forward a century or so. Movies and television always have been viewed with suspicion by Christians who have argued that they depict and glamorize immorality even though, until 1966, Hollywood had a production code which restricted obscene language, sex, violence, religious ridicule, ethnic insults, drug abuse and other offensive portrayals. In order to help Christians with their viewing choices, the Catholic Legion of Decency began awarding movies moral ratings in 1936, and the Protestant Motion Picture Council was set up in 1944.

More recently there has been a battle with popular music, particularly African American music such as jazz, blues and hip-hop. The Christian opposition to rock 'n' roll has gone though several distinct phases involving record burnings, demonstrations and boycotts.

Initially the fears were racial and sexual. Some white people worried that the acceptance of black music by their teenagers would increase the possibility of racial integration. (If they liked their music they might start liking them!) They were also worried that the music might arouse sexual passions because the driving rhythms encouraged physical abandonment.

When desegregation was introduced and the war in Vietnam escalated, the fear became political rebellion. One Christian writer, David A. Noebel, wrote two books, *Rhythm, Riots and Revolution*[9] and *Communism, Hypnotism and the Beatles*,[10] in which he claimed that rock 'n' roll was being used by Russian communists to inflict psychological and moral damage on America's young people as part of a subtle softening up procedure.

With the end of the war and the fragmentation of the radical political movements, the communist plot theory withered only to be replaced by the devil's music theory, which postulated that some rock 'n' roll derived its power from the occult. This was seemingly proved by tape recordings of particular album tracks which, when played backwards, contained messages encouraging listeners to follow Satan.

The association of music with social disorder and spirit possession has a long history. The great virtuoso Niccolo Paganini, who toured Britain in the 1830s, played his violin at such a speed that people said that they could see the devil standing at his elbow. A century later the blues guitarist Robert Johnson was rumored to have acquired his talent after making a pact with the devil. At different times both the fiddle and the guitar have been regarded as special tools of evil.

This attitude has created difficulties for young people raised in church. Often those who decided to make careers out of rock 'n' roll did so convinced that they alienated themselves from God. Some even began to live in ways that seemed appropriate to such a rebellion. Jerry Lee Lewis, cousin of televangelist Jimmy Swaggart, said that he thought he was "dragging the audience to hell" when he played. Elvis Presley worried throughout his life that he had missed his calling as a gospel singer.

Modern Catholics often haven't encountered the same apprehensions about art as Protestant evangelicals. The Roman Catholic Church has been much more ready to celebrate its artists. The postconciliar Vatican II document, "Pastoral Constitution of the Church in the Modern World" (1965), stated:

> In their own way literature and art are very important in the life of the Church. They seek to give expression to man's nature, his problems and his experience in an effort to discover and perfect man himself and the world in which he lives; they try to discover his place in

history and in the universe, to throw light on his suffering and his joy, his needs and potentialities, and to outline a happier destiny in store for him. Hence they can elevate human life, which they express under many forms according to various times and places.

In cinema there have been far more sympathetically portrayed Catholic priests and nuns than there have been Protestant pastors or evangelists. Three of Hollywood's most acclaimed directors—Frank Capra, Alfred Hitchcock and John Ford—were all practicing Catholics. The French director Robert Bresson, recognized by some as the most Catholic of filmmakers, said that he wanted his work to make a person's soul and the presence of God perceptible to an audience.

In literature there are many examples of highly regarded and influential novelists who were members of the Roman Catholic Church: Evelyn Waugh and Graham Greene in England, Walker Percy and Flannery O'Connor in America, François Mauriac and Georges Bernanos in France, Shusaku Endo in Japan. Each of them, in different ways, explored the tensions created through living by faith in a world where faith has largely been lost.

Why should this be so? Why have Catholics not only experienced more liberty in the arts but been able to reach the general public rather than a specialized Christian market? Often Catholics who have lost their faith incorporate more pertinent theological issues into their work than Protestants who haven't. "There is no such thing as a Protestant Novel, as far as I know," said American novelist Coleman Dowell in 1978. "But, if there were, wouldn't it be dull? No Protestant novelist writes from being a Protestant."[11]

There seem to be a number of contributing factors, and these could equally well apply to the Orthodox churches of Russia and Greece which produced such writers as Tolstoy, Dostoyevsky and Kazantzakis. First, the Catholic Church, as we have already seen, has had a long history of honoring artists and craftsmen and didn't suffer the anxieties of the Puritans over the validity of the arts. The original audience for Shakespeare's plays most likely consisted of a high proportion of Catholics because of Puritan distaste for plays. A lot of evidence points to Shakespeare himself, while a Protestant in practice, being Catholic in sympathy.

Second, and closely related, is the fact that the worship experience offered to Catholics is theatrical and sensual: the sight of processionals, colored robes, mitres, flickering candles, stained glass and sacred art, the sound of chanting and singing, the smell of incense, the taste of bread and wine, the touch of priests' hands. Cardinal John Henry Newman, a nineteenth-century convert from Anglicanism, wrote:

> The Catholic Church is the poet of her children, full of music to soothe the sad and control the wayward, wonderful in story for the imagination of the romantic, rich in symbol and imagery, so that gentle and delicate feelings, which will not bear words, may in silence intimate their presence or commune with themselves. Her very being is poetry; every psalm, every petition, every collect, every versicle, the cross, the mitre, the thurible, is a fulfilment of some dream of childhood or aspiration of youth.[12]

Catholics who become artists frequently credit the church for their first aesthetic experiences. Filmmaker Martin Scorcese remembers being taken to Mass as a child:

> It was so impressive, with different colored vestments for the different Masses: white and gold, or green and gold. I guess I made the association between going to the cathedral and to the movie theater at an early age. In fact, as kids we used to joke about Mass being the same show every day.[13]

Third, Roman Catholicism emphasizes the sacramental. Bread and wine, oil and ash, water and flame can all become channels of grace. In a similar way, God can confront us through ordinary people, things or events. What this means for Catholic artists is that they are prepared to see a second dimension to the commonplace. They are ready to see the infinite working through the finite. In fiction this provides the opportunity for a deluge of rain, for example, to be interpreted as either a divine punishment (as with Noah) or a form of cleansing (like baptism). The stuff of life becomes charged with possibilities. "The real novelist," wrote Flannery O'Connor, "the one with an instinct for what he is about, knows that he cannot approach the infinite directly, that he must penetrate the natural human world as it is. The more sacramental his theology, the more encouragement he will get from it to do just that."[14]

Fourth, the practice of self-examination and confession to a priest acts as a good discipline for thinking about motives and speaking about human folly. The learning of the catechism at an early age also seems to impress the basics of theology so deeply that even if the artist later disowns the faith, the residual doctrine continues to exercise a powerful effect. Although the beat novelist Jack Kerouac had stopped attending church by the time he wrote his first book, his writing nevertheless was permeated with a lingering Catholicism, and he in fact preferred to be thought of as a " strange solitary crazy Catholic mystic" rather than as the father of the Beats.

Fifth, Catholicism was ahead of evangelical Protestantism in arts scholarship. When films, novels and art exhibitions are reviewed and discussed in church and seminary magazines, it creates an environment where creativity is accepted and where it seems natural for church members to want to become artists. The Catholic journal *Jubilee* featured interviews with artists in the 1960s. *The Critic* began running extracts from fiction and short stories. Yet some of the same problems affecting Protestantism must have remained, for in 1961 Flannery O'Connor complained that "fiction is considered by most Catholic readers to be a waste of time."

The problem that has affected the church down through the ages with regard to art can be put very simply: How much of life is Christ to be Lord over? Is he only interested in that part of life we think of as religious or spiritual? Or is he interested in every facet of our lives—body, soul, mind and spirit? The sort of art we make as Christians will illustrate our answer.

three

the world

To the contemporary mind, particularly to the mind of the contemporary artist, the sins that concerned our Christian ancestors are of no consequence. Idolatry, triviality, worldliness—who cares? Progress is measured by the number of prohibitions that can be thrown off. Concern over moral minutiae is regarded on an individual level as a neurosis and on a collective level as a failure to modernize.

Not surprisingly, Christians in the arts who have felt impeded by wrong-headed applications of biblical principles are tempted to follow suit. They want to give up thinking too deeply about what is right and wrong. It has become too much of a struggle. They are already misunderstood by the secular world because of their faith and now they're misunderstood by the church because of their art. For them the safest way ahead seems to be to hold on to a minimum of doctrine and avoid getting too anxious over the purity of their work.

However, as Christians we can't blithely dismiss the convictions of those from another age on the grounds that we know better because we live in the twenty-first century. Being less affected by secular humanism, our ancestors may have had a clearer view. They certainly held their beliefs with as much or more sincerity and integrity as we hold ours. We should at least listen to them.

The making of "graven images" was the original issue in debates about Christianity and art, yet it is clear from Exodus 20 that art only becomes an idol when it replaces God. This was the view of the Puritan Thomas Watson, who wrote in the seventeenth century, "In the first commandment worshipping a false god is forbidden; in this (the second), worshipping the true God in a false manner . . . It forbids not the making of an image for civil use."[1] Jesus noted the image of Caesar's head on a Roman coin without accusing the coin-bearer of idolatry (Matthew 22:21).

Few in the West today bow before three-dimensional objects, but there is a related issue that should concern Christians. In a secular society, art itself can be the subject of a religious type of devotion. It's common to hear artists talk of their work as being their religion—their personal salvation and also their hope for the world. "Given the ever-present absence of God," concluded the atheist art critic Peter Fuller, "art, and the gamut of aesthetic experience, provides the sole remaining glimmer of transcendence."[2]

The movie director, actor and rock star are far more readily listened to than the preacher or theologian. We know more pop songs than hymns, more movie plots than Bible stories. There is more fanfare surrounding the opening of a new city art gallery than the dedication of a new church or cathedral. Even a critical appreciation of Shakespeare is considered more essential to a cultured mind than an understanding of Pauline theology.

The modern temptation is to make art with the intention that it becomes idolized. Rock stars, in particular, are often keen to appear to be in possession of special knowledge and deliberately manufacture mystique. But it wouldn't be right for a Christian performer to create this sort of impression. If the Son of God was not aloof and was humble enough to wash the feet of his disciples, and if Paul disabused those who mistook him for a Greek god by shouting, "We too are only men, human like you" (Acts 14:15), how can a humble musician be justified in promoting the idea of the superiority of the performer over members of the audience?

Our Christian ancestors also worried about art portraying sin or things that might lead people to sin, even if only in thought. This still presents Christians with a dilemma. The most obvious example, and one that the Puritans would frequently cite with regard to the theater, was the portrayal of adultery. How could a Christian be edified while being entertained by the sight of two people enacting the breaking of one of the Ten Commandments?

The twentieth-century American evangelist Billy Sunday, whose preaching career took off at around the same time as Hollywood was developing, once said, "We are flooded with the vile drama that mocks and scoffs at the sacredness of marriage and now we have the immoral picture shows. You go to see a musical comedy and there you see a girl that hasn't enough clothes on to flag a hand car, and they try to hide behind the word art."[3]

Adultery, violence, murder, deceit, fornication, betrayal and pride are clearly important to adult storytelling, whether in fiction, in film or on the stage. A simplistic reading of the situation would conclude that these sins are included to appeal to the base in human nature. Sometimes they are. But it is often more deep rooted than that. Drama depends on conflict. The protagonist must face tests and trials and through overcoming them, reveal his or her true character. Violence and sexual betrayal are among the most extreme tests we can face, which is why they are so frequently used in story lines.

The Old Testament king David's character was revealed when he came within easy reach of his enemy King Saul and had a sharpened sword in his hand. He could have killed Saul, but he chose instead to cut a section of his robe because he respected Saul's role as king. David's character was also revealed when he spied Bathsheba naked on a rooftop. In order to get her for himself he had her husband killed. These are the extreme tests that make drama compelling.

If the obstacles the writer introduces either don't seem challenging enough (for example, the protagonist is handed back too much change in a store and worries about whether to return it) or don't seem real enough (for example, a fight ensues but no punches are seen to land and no blood is spilled), then evil doesn't appear evil enough, and if good triumphs, it won't appear good enough. This is why so much "Christian fiction" lacks the ring of truth. The action doesn't appear to take place in the "real world."

Mindful of his Calvinistic heritage Daniel Defoe argued in the preface to *Moll Flanders*: "To give the history of a wicked life repented of, necessarily requires that the wicked part should be made as wicked as the real history of it will bear, to illustrate and give beauty to the penitent part, which is certainly the best and brightest, if related with equal spirit and life."[4] François Mauriac said that his job as a novelist was to make evil "perceptible, tangible, odorous. The theologian gives us an abstract idea of the sinner. I give him flesh and blood."[5] Or, as John Henry Cardinal Newman once observed, "It is a contradiction in terms to attempt a sinless literature of sinful man."

Yet how can this be reconciled with Paul's advice in Philippians 4:8 when he writes, "Whatever is true, whatever is noble, whatever is right, whatever is pure, whatever is lovely, whatever is admirable—if anything is excellent and praiseworthy—think about such things"?

This verse, probably more than any other, has been used to deter Christians from the arts. It has been interpreted as meaning only look at, listen to or read things which are noble, right, pure, lovely, admirable, excellent or praiseworthy. Yet this would preclude us from passing our eyes over much of the descriptions of impurity and awfulness in the Bible. David's life would have to be read in an abridged version. Could we dwell on Job or Revelation? How could we deal with the negativity in Ecclesiastes?

A corollary of this has been that Christians have thought that they should only create art with a Pollyanna quality to it: paintings of birds and kittens, movies that extol family life and end happily, songs that are positive and uplifting—in short, works of art that show a world that is almost unfallen where no one experiences conflict and where sin is naughty rather than wicked.

I believe that Paul is saying something else. First, he is listing the standards by which we should judge all that we see, think and do. As we read *Macbeth*, for example, we hold nobility and purity as our ideals and we measure the characters against them. What we find is that although the play involves murder, deceit, pride and betrayal, the main sinners fall victim to their sins and the Christian values of nobility, purity, truth and faithfulness triumph.

Paul, who was schooled in Greek culture, was not expecting us only to expose ourselves to the thoughts and ideas of our fellow Christians. Truth is not exclusive to believers. We accept this in areas such as medicine, cartography and space exploration but begrudgingly in philosophy, psychology and the arts. Christians sometimes reason that if unbelievers are "darkened in their understanding and separated from the life of God" (Ephesians 4:18) they can never come up with any accurate insights into the human condition.

When Paul spoke of darkened understanding he was speaking specifically of the inability of the sinner to respond to God affirmatively without being spiritually awakened. He didn't imply that these people were incapable of evaluating information, conducting accurate research or being creatively inspired.

The role of truth in the life of the Christian can be confusing. Christ told his disciples that they would "know the truth, and the truth will set you free" (John 8:32). This can lead to two false conclusions: one, that the Christian knows the truth about everything, and two, that the non-Christian doesn't know the truth about anything. These naturally result in arrogance.

The truth that sets us free is not human wisdom but Christ, the Living Truth. It is he who liberates us from sin and death, but he doesn't promise an automatic advantage in all areas of truth. The truth that Jesus promised the Holy Spirit would lead us into (John

16:12) didn't involve the truth about physics, geology, astronomy and sociology, and yet we are privileged to know truths about our origin, purpose and destiny which couldn't be discovered in any way other than through divine revelation.

Second, Paul is telling us what values should always remain uppermost in our thoughts. When we read of David's adultery we judge him to be wrong because he was impure, but when we close the Bible it is the standard of purity that remains with us, not the infidelity and deceit. When we read of the betrayal carried out by Judas, we judge him by the standards of nobility.

Some art is so obviously and thoroughly inspired by evil that we can't benefit from it at all. Some art leaves us with images that we find hard to erase or words that come back to haunt us. In my lifetime I have seen Christians go from an almost total ban on movie-going to a laissez-faire attitude that we can watch anything as long as we have an appropriate comment to make at the end. We should respect the power of art. We can't let our spirits take any amount of punishment and expect to emerge unscathed. Sometimes we give ourselves permission to watch, listen or read such material because we say it's "just for a laugh" or "a bit of fun." But that usually means that our critical faculties are relaxed, and it is precisely at these times that our thinking can be shaped by ideas that are antagonistic towards faithful living. I think that T. S. Eliot had it right when he concluded that "it is just the literature that we read for 'amusement,' or 'purely for pleasure' that may have the greatest and least suspected influence upon us. It is the literature that we read with the least effort that can have the easiest and most insidious influence upon us."[6]

A related objection is that the arts are often an invitation to worldly thinking. Arguments that we would challenge if put to us as verbal propositions are approached less critically when they come to us as art or entertainment. We are softened up through a steady diet of movies, songs, novels and television, which implicitly deny our most cherished beliefs.

The Bible does warn against the "world" and "worldliness" and so if we are to be faithful we have to find out what that means. Extremism comes from confusing two biblical usages of the word *world*. On the one hand, there is the created world that God deemed "good," which is contrasted with the rest of the universe. "For God so loved the world" is as much a statement about our globe, distinguished from the rest of the universe, as it is about love. On the other hand, there is the rebellious system of thinking we might contrast with the kingdom of heaven. "Love not the world" means neither "Don't care for the planet" nor "Drop out of society," but "Don't embrace anti-God thinking."

Confusing these two usages can lead to disaster. Some strict fundamentalist sects show disdain toward creation and culture, and yet in doing so become proud, arrogant and uncaring. They therefore become worldly in the very way the Bible condemns and yet are not worldly enough in the way the Bible commands. We are told to be in the world but not of it. People like this are often of the world but not in it.

Richard Lovelace, in his classic study *Dynamics of Spiritual Life*, sums up the world in its negative sense as "the total system of corporate flesh operating on earth under satanic control, with all its incentives of reward and restraints of loss, its characteristic patterns of behavior, and its antichristian structures, methods, goals and ideologies."[7]

We become worldly not by engaging with the world but by allowing it to shape our thinking. Jesus was clear about this. His prayer for his disciples was "not that you take them out of the world but that you protect them from the evil one" (John 17:15). Paul underscored it. He reminded the Corinthians that his warning not to associate with the sexually immoral, the greedy, swindlers and idolaters was "not at all meaning the people of this world." Why? Because if he had meant that, "You would have to leave this world" (1 Corinthians 5:9-11). His warning was against fraternizing with those calling themselves Christians who lived this way.

The art of nonbelievers, like the friendship of nonbelievers, could be part of a process pressing us to conform to the "pattern of this world" as Paul called it in Romans, but it doesn't have to be if we are being transformed through godly mind renewal. In fact, wrestling with worldly ideas is one way in which our minds are renewed. It challenges our assumptions and threatens our complacency. It sends us back to the Bible and forces us to kneel in prayer.

Having a renewed mind doesn't mean that we become spiritually invincible. It's my renewed mind that urges me to switch off certain TV talk shows when I realize that I'm actually enjoying the humiliation of the guest and the bloodlust of the audience. It's my renewed mind that warns me that certain volumes of theology may encourage my doubts rather than build my assurance.

Positively, the world is all that God made and Christ came to redeem. This includes culture because humans have never lived in isolation from each other, and when they get together they automatically create culture. It would be impossible to think of loving humans and yet hating human culture, of loving individuals and yet hating their music, songs, stories, paintings, games, rituals, decorations, clothes, languages and hairstyles. God made us cultural beings.

Therefore, Christians should be worldly in this positive sense. They should be lovers of life because God is the giver of life. No one is more worldly than God—he made the world, upholds the world and sent his Son to die for the world. Christianity doesn't teach that the world is an illusion that will trap us or a hell that prevents us from attaining our true purpose.

The third worry about secular art has been that it is trivial. If we believe we are participants in a struggle, how can we spend time in leisurely contemplation of paintings or relaxing with a CD? Don't the New Testament analogies of the Christian life as a war or a race show that we have no time to slow down and relax?

Not everything in our lives is equally pressing and vital. We couldn't live that way. Intense moments have to be followed by times of restoration; we suffer ill health if we don't get this rhythm right. Jesus ministered, preached and healed, but he also walked, drank and ate. He spoke to crowds, but he also relaxed with friends.

The writer Tom Howard, in his excellent memoir *Christ the Tiger*, tells of Christian colleges in the early 1960s that placed strictures on films and records because they didn't contribute to a robust spiritual life. "But," thought Howard, "do doughnuts? Or roller coaster rides? Or hootenannies?"[8] In the words of the Teacher, "There is a time for everything, and a season for every activity under heaven . . . a time to weep and a time to laugh, a time to mourn and a time to dance" (Ecclesiastes 3:1, 4).

Art blesses in ways that are hard to quantify. Bruno Bettleheim, in his book *The Uses of Enchantment*,[9] argues that stories help children cope with the complexities of life. Medical studies show that laughter and music help us deal with stress. Painting and photography deepen our appreciation of light, color and detail. Dance makes us aware of the form and movement of the human body. A life without art would be harsh, dull and difficult.

Yet it's not because we can prove that art has benefits that we feel able to incorporate it into our lives. It should be part of the warp and woof of our existence, a part of our enjoyment of God. It is not something separate from life, but something at the heart of life which celebrates the fact that we are creator children of a creator Father.

The criticism that art involves falsehood quite rightly doesn't trouble people today. Those who condemned novels for being untrue had failed to distinguish between illusion and deceit. Art depends on illusion: paintings use perspective to give the illusion of depth, movies use fast frames to give the illusion of movement, singers give the illusion of experiencing heartbreak or joy as they sing, actors give the illusion of being people that they are not. But those who experience these art forms know that they are submitting to an illusion; they are not deceived.

There is no reason to insist that the parables Jesus told were accounts of actual events. They were stories told to illustrate truths, just as stories that begin with "A man went into a bar" are usually told to create laughter. In both cases the audience is familiar with the form and is not expecting to hear a factual report. So when Jesus said, "There was a man who had two sons . . . " it could be said that he was leading people to believe a lie. But we know that the truth in the parable of the son who returns to his father after frittering away his inheritance is theological rather than historical.

By far the most persistent criticism of art made by Christians is that unless it is done for the church it is secular, and if it is secular it cannot be done to the glory of God. When I was researching my book *Trouble Man: The Life and Death of Marvin Gaye*[10] I visited an African American church in Kentucky where one of the pastors asked me this question: "Gospel music is made for the glory of God but for whose glory is pop music made?"

I assumed I was meant to think that if someone wasn't singing about God, they couldn't be singing to God's glory and that if they weren't singing for God's glory then they must be singing to the glory of the devil. It's a tortured logic but one I have seen affect some of the most innovative artists in rock music. It can lead people to think that they are damned for singing a song about the joy of being in love or driving a fast car.

Although my questioner wouldn't have been aware of it, he was the recipient of a doctrine with a history predating Christianity, a doctrine that separates body and mind from spirit and soul, and which has had a lot to do with the present low profile of Christians in the mainstream arts.

four

the split

A	*key issue in the strained relationship between Christianity* and the arts is the perceived division between secular and sacred. Christians have found it hard to appreciate art that deals with daily living, especially if it doesn't supply an obviously spiritual conclusion.

This problem is exemplified in what is known as contemporary Christian music (CCM). Created as a marketing category to distinguish what had once been known as Jesus rock from traditional southern gospel, it is music created by Christians and largely consumed by Christians. As far as I am aware, it is the only musical category recognized in the record industry that is defined entirely by lyrical content. All other categories—blues, soul, dance, heavy metal, rap and so on—are defined by musical style.

This criterion has naturally focused attention on the words of the songs at the expense of the quality of musical composition, musicianship and studio production. CCM practitioners are judged by the pungency of their message and remain eligible for the genre only as long as their lyrics fall inside prescribed parameters. Many of them refer to their work not as an art but as a ministry and speak openly about using their music "to reach the world for Christ."

For many Christians, preaching is the role model for communica-tion and the arts are simply another form of communication. Conse-quently they create art that involves a clearly understood message and possibly even a challenge. The listener is not meant to be enriched but changed. Success is gauged not in terms of critical appreciation but in souls saved.

The thinking behind creating such music seems to be as follows: Young people today don't have high regard for preachers, and yet they do emulate rock stars. Some rock music contains thought-provoking lyrics. Therefore, the Christian gospel, if successfully couched in a rock music setting, could be more effective among youth than if it was declared from a pulpit.

This is faulty thinking. It confuses the power of the Spirit with the power of technology, charisma and mystique. Rock music can have power over people for reasons that range from the decibel level to the image of a singer built up through the media. The popular mes-sages put over by rock music are usually popular not because they reverse the direction of society, but because they encourage the direction it is already going in.

Nowhere was this more clearly emphasized than when I saw Bob Dylan perform his first concerts with songs written out of an experi-ence of Jesus. On paper this was the perfect opportunity to see a generation influenced by the gospel. Here was one of the most pow-erful icons from the baby-boom generation pleading with his audi-ence to "get ready," "wake up" and "serve the Lord." The result at the concert I attended in San Francisco was that the audience jeered, walked out or demanded to hear his old material. Reviewers were equally condemning. This was not the message that they wanted to hear. They wanted their worldviews to be endorsed, not brought into question, and no amount of charisma, artistic talent and status could change that.

The power of effective preaching isn't a question of art. Preachers should of course be well read, skillful with language, aware of intonation and able to craft arguments that engage the interest of the ordinary person, but if we could explain a revival in terms of artistry, then we would be right to credit the artists and not the Spirit. Success in preaching is not a simple matter of effective communication.

Jonathan Edwards, the great preacher of the New England revival, achieved spectacular effects although he read his sermons and did it in a quiet voice. When the evangelist D. L. Moody came to Britain in the 1870s, what surprised those who saw him was that there seemed to be nothing in his disposition or style that could explain the power that was unleashed when he preached. Moody, for his part, was greatly pleased to know that what he did couldn't be analyzed in human terms.

It is therefore wrong for Christians to think that if only we could employ the most powerful arts and media available today we could bring about conversions on a scale never seen before. The power of Steven Spielberg the filmmaker to sell cinema seats or Madonna the musician to sell CDs would not be automatically translated into the power to save souls should they choose to give their gift to the Lord. They may be listened to by more people, for a short while at least, but if they were to be explicit about the Christian faith they would face the same indifference or resistance that any other proclaimer of the good news has encountered.

When Christians think of the arts as something that can be used to win the world to Christ, they create an unrealistic expectation of the arts and put unfair pressure on artists. Christian songwriters are automatically expected to write "Christian songs." But what constitutes a "Christian song"? In theory, according to the Gospel Music Association, a gospel song can be in any style as long as it contains worship or testimony, or is "informed by a Christian worldview." In practice, it tends to be a song that contains the requisite amount of references to the Lord, God, Jesus or the Spirit. Otherwise, how would a half-attentive radio audience know it was listening to CCM?

Frequently a "Christian worldview" is interpreted to mean a view of a pressing moral problem broadly accepted by evangelicals. Therefore, a song protesting abortion or pornography would fulfill the criteria. A song recommending the cancellation of third-world debt might not because, although the idea of this sort of debt cancellation is derived from Old Testament practices, it can seem too political. So already the definition of a "Christian worldview" is problematic.

However, the truly Christian worldview is far more pervasive and often less obviously religious than people imagine. Many assumptions in our culture are rooted in the Bible. The dignity of labor and the responsibility for nurturing our talents are biblical views. Concern for an impartial judicial system is biblical. Respect for parents is biblical. I'm not sure that a song that dignified the work of a street sweeper would be considered "Christian" by the CCM industry.

Then there are areas of daily living where the experience of the Christian is no different from that of the agnostic, atheist or believer in false gods. For example, I like relaxing in a warm bath. If I were to discuss this with anyone, regardless of belief, they would at least know what I meant even if they didn't share my enthusiasm. Uniting us would be our common humanity. We all laugh, cry, eat, sleep and sweat, and some of us take baths.

My perspective on the joy of warm baths, if I cared to elaborate, would be different because of my faith. I may take less of them because I am concerned about wasting natural resources. I may lie back and offer a prayer of thanks for the good things in life. I would of course believe that God created both water and the materials for the bathtub. But if I were conversing with someone about this pleasure I wouldn't feel compelled to include this information in the conversation.

Similarly, in writing songs the stuff of human life is the artist's resource. The Beatles wrote about bed ("I'm Only Sleeping"), boredom ("Good Morning"), nostalgia ("In My Life"), childhood

("Penny Lane"), the weather ("Rain"), loneliness ("Eleanor Rigby") and money ("Taxman"), among other subjects. They were under no pressure to summarize their life philosophy in a single song and yet, if you were to collect their songs and piece them together like a jigsaw puzzle, you could discover a life philosophy, or at least part of one.

Christian songwriters are encouraged to ignore the ordinary things of life because they don't provide the opportunity to witness. Mention of soup or football doesn't naturally lead to Calvary. They are then left with the overtly spiritual, and this has the effect of making them seem out of balance to non-Christian observers. It appears that they have no regular life, that they don't inhabit the normal world of telephones, cars, surf, television, mountains and fast food. They are like the people who can only talk about how good the Lord has been but can't hold a conversation about baseball, the weather, the economy, the price of gas or the state of education.

The gospel is not limited to mentions of the death, resurrection and ascension of Jesus. That, of course, is the hub of the matter. There would be no good news without it. But in its fullness, the gospel spreads out and embraces all aspects of our lives. It includes the renewed mind that Paul refers to, the wisdom sought after by Solomon and the justice called for by Amos.

C. S. Lewis once said that he believed in God like he believed in the sun: "Not because I can see him, but because by him I can see everything else." It is possible to create work saturated with gospel insights without spelling out the plan of salvation, just as it is possible to demonstrate the joys of a loving marriage without showing off your wedding photographs. Songwriter T. Bone Burnett, speaking to the *L. A. Weekly*, said, "If Jesus is the Light of the World, there are two kinds of songs you can write. You can write songs about the light, or you can write songs about what you can see from the light. That's what I try to do."

The need to witness in art is nothing more than an application in one particular area of what we are told to do in general. All Christians should believe in making disciples, but just as a doctor would not be expected to preach to patients or a plumber to wrap texts around new pipe work so artists shouldn't be required to turn their occupation into full-time evangelism unless specifically called to do so.

By continuously "praising the Lord" the CCM artist rarely shows evidence of a comprehensive worldview. In fact, the world is not viewed at all. What is viewed is personal spiritual experience and usually only its more beautiful peaks. The valley of the shadow of death is rarely traversed, nor is the valley of indecision. The casual nonbelieving browser is effectively excluded because there is no overlap of experience.

This raises the question of the relationship between art and propaganda. Some might argue that it is perfectly legitimate to use a song, novel or play as a type of sermon because art has frequently been used to move people to change their opinions. Looking at rock music alone, there have been songs urging us to love everyone ("All You Need Is Love," Beatles), songs selling the virtues of atheism ("Imagine," John Lennon), songs attacking the British monarchy ("God Save The Queen," Sex Pistols) and songs denouncing apartheid ("Sun City," Artists United Against Apartheid). The poetry and plays of Bertolt Brecht in the 1930s were written against fascism. Picasso painted *Guernica* to show the horrors of the Spanish Civil War. Arthur Miller wrote his play *The Crucible* because he was angered by the trials of suspected communists in American public life organized by Senator Joe McCarthy.

Art can be used to persuade. But acknowledging this is not to conclude that art can only be justified if it used in this way. Art is created from passion, and when artists are passionate about injustice or persecution it is almost inevitable that it will affect their work. Usually, however, these people are not single-issue artists. Picasso's feelings about the destruction of Guernica can be seen alongside his feelings about everything from music to women to food to death. Arthur Miller didn't return to the subject of the McCarthy witch-hunt.

It should also be remembered that art created to change minds often actually does more to bolster the spirit of those already in agreement than it does to convert opponents. The antiwar songs of the 1960s put into words the ideas of the young people opposed to American engagement in Vietnam, but had no reported impact on the policymakers inside the Pentagon.

When art is given over to propaganda it tends to lose the human dimension because it is consumed by the issue. It oversimplifies complex issues. It vilifies the enemy. It devalues words and images. For examples of this we can look at the art approved by the Nazi Party in Germany during the 1930s and the official art of Russia under communism. Significantly, the only art that has survived from this period that still moves people is the art that was then suppressed and which challenged the orthodoxy of the day.

Some art is simply playful. It may be about nothing more than itself. It attempts neither to tell a story or to make a point. A photographer's eye is caught by the peeling paint on the door of a Mediterranean cottage. A poet toys with a combination of words that seems both magical and musical. A painter experiments with color and texture with all the joy of a child playing in a mud bath. A sculptor makes a three-dimensional pun.

To some Christians this is a wasted opportunity, a sermon with no content, a Bible exposition with no substance. But playfulness is an important component of art and perfectly in keeping with a Christian understanding of creativity. Look at the animal kingdom. Can't we sense a spirit of playfulness in the designs? Watching fish from the windows of an underwater observatory in the Red Sea recently I was struck first by the incredible array of colors and then by what I think can only be described as God's humor. The flattened out shapes, the bulging lips, the hammer heads—it was like looking at the sketch pad of someone who had come up with a basic design and was having fun creating as many variations as possible. "God,"

Picasso once said, "is really only another artist. He invented the giraffe, the elephant, and the cat. He has no real style. He just keeps trying other things."

The sound of words can inspire songwriters before a meaning becomes apparent. Sometimes there is no obvious meaning and sometimes there are several possible meanings. Dummy lyrics, used while a song is being composed without any thought to literal sense, often become so molded to the music that it doesn't seem worth improving them. Singer-songwriter Beck typifies this approach when he says, "I sculpt the words, but they also have to feel good in a melody. Sometimes, I'll put in a line just because it suits the melody. It won't be something that speaks of the emotional core in me, but I can't change it as it goes with the melody so much. You can go for the most expensive, crafted shirt in the world, but you're still going to prefer the one that feels good when you wear it. That's what I go for in a song. Ultimately, does it feel good to listen to?"

Because they are forced to work within narrow parameters, CCM artists are disadvantaged. While their non-Christian contemporaries work to create music which makes people go "Wow! Play that again. I love it," they are having to come up with lyric-driven songs presumably designed to make people say, "That's interesting. I agree with that sentiment. That seems true." I suspect that I'm not alone in listening to songs because they excite, relax, console or uplift me rather than because they contain words that endorse certain of my convictions.

Songwriting, like all the arts, should involve self-discovery. As it has been said, "How can I know what I think until I see what I write?" The artist taps deep levels of consciousness and brings to the surface things that amaze him or her. A lot of CCM songwriting begins with a conclusion and the lyric is simply used to expound it. There is no sense of revelation because the artist wasn't on a voyage of discovery. There are no surprises because the artist wasn't surprised. Arthur Miller has said:

For myself, it has never been possible to generate the energy to write and complete a play if I know in advance everything it signifies and all it will contain. The very impulse to write, I think, springs from an inner chaos crying for order, for meaning, and that meaning, must be discovered in the process of writing or the work lies dead as it is finished. To speak, therefore, of a play as though it were the objective work of a propagandist is an almost biological kind of nonsense, provided, of course, that it is a play, which is to say a work of art.[1]

The Scottish poet and musician Don Paterson (not a Christian, as far as I know) says that poems should either surprise or frighten the poet who is writing them. He argues that the poet should be hit by words (just as I assume he would expect a musician to be hit by sounds) and it is from these words that some sense may later emerge.

I don't think poets get ideas for poems, they get words; that's their gift, and they forget it at their peril. What usually happens (to me) is that I get this phrase in my head that I can't leave alone; sometimes it's original, sometimes a cliche or some bit of received language I've discovered something new in; it constantly surprises me when I think about it and that's completely essential—if it doesn't surprise me, I can't expect it to surprise the reader, which is the whole point of the exercise.[2]

A sermon requires authority, clarity and a personal challenge. Art, on the other hand, often deals in doubt, ambiguity and self-criticism. The Irish poet W. B. Yeats once observed that the quarrel with others produced rhetoric but the quarrel with oneself produced poetry.[3] So often Christian artists feel that their role is to take on the enemy, whereas they would produce better and more accessible work if they dealt with the contradictions, waverings and weaknesses within themselves.

The demand for overtly religious lyrics doesn't only come from the Christian music industry. The audience judges artists by their words. If a musician has too many songs without the requisite buzz words, they are thought to have lost the faith or at least be in a period of "backsliding." I've known musicians who haven't supplied the correct number of references to Jesus to receive letters beginning, "Dear former brother in Christ." Conversely, if a well-known mainstream artist makes even a passing reference to "the Lord" they will be claimed as a believer by an audience desperate to have famous people counted among their number.

Musicians in the Christian music industry who stop using enough religious words are said to have gone secular, and this is not meant in a positive way. However, the description *secular* is very much like *world* in that it has two very different connotations. We may use it to mean nonreligious, in the sense of having no transcendent dimension. Secular humanism is a view of the world that doesn't include God. A secular society likewise is based on atheistic or agnostic principles. We may also use *secular* to mean nonreligious in the sense of those things that take place outside of such spiritual activities as praying, worshiping, witnessing, ministering and reading the Bible. Understood in this way, attending church on a Sunday is a religious activity but playing sport on a Saturday is a secular activity.

But there is no natural connection between activities that take place outside of church and denying God. *Secular* simply means "of this temporal world or age," and most of the things that dominate our lives are necessarily of this temporal world or age and none the worse for being so. Of course, for a nonbeliever, secular activities are viewed in a secular way, but a believer should view secular activities as part of a spiritual life. The strength, wisdom and guidance gained during the small portion of our lives we think of as religious should percolate through the larger portion of our lives we think of as secular. "So whether you eat or drink or whatever you do, do it all for the glory of God" (1 Corinthians 10:31).

Christians who categorize art as secular if it isn't explicitly religious often either refuse to make it because they think it is a compromise or they go ahead and make it but imagine that they are entering a faith-free zone. I once saw a poet's entry in a directory of Christian artists which said: "I write poems both Christian and non-Christian." I presume that he meant that the subject matter of some of his poetry was obviously religious and some of it wasn't, but the choice of phrase (from a poet too!) betrayed an attitude that he himself had perhaps not recognized.

The Bible has no equivalent division between secular and religious in the believer's life because anything good in the temporal world can be "set apart for God," in other words made sacred. Marriage, which we are told will not extend to the afterlife and is therefore "of this temporal age," can be made holy. Child rearing can be done in a godly way. Even taking food and drink can, as we have already seen, be done in a spiritual way.

Christians are often affected by the idea that the otherworldly (heaven, the spiritual realms) is the big deal and that everything earthly (work, leisure) is tawdry. This life is a vale of tears which we are to tolerate but not enjoy. The only relief comes when we can think about God and his angels. There is even a chorus which says:

Turn your eyes upon Jesus
Look full in his wonderful face
And the things of earth will grow strangely dim
In the light of his glory and grace.[4]

The writer may well have meant that our earthly problems are put into perspective when we look to Jesus, but it can appear to mean that our nonreligious experiences should be dimmed. This can lead people to wonder why God bothered to create the physical world and its enjoyments if we can only be truly fulfilled by escaping them.

If we believe that this world is unreal, if our wish is that the things of this life should "grow strangely dim," then we have developed a dualistic view of life. We are not seeing the important division as that which exists between righteousness and evil but between the material and the nonmaterial. With this perspective, body-based activities such as sport or sex are regarded as inferior to spirit-based activities such as worship and meditation.

We do not need to overtly refer to God in everything we create. Not even every book in the Bible refers to God. Jesus surely didn't mark all his carpentry with a relevant saying, and Paul didn't embroider memory verses on his tents. Christians need wisdom to know when it is appropriate to introduce mention of God or Jesus Christ. There is nothing more disconcerting than when an engaging piece of work suddenly lurches into explicit theology without any apparent connection. It's as if the author has discharged a responsibility rather than reached a natural conclusion.

Some art needs to stick to its subject and not attempt any leaps of logic in order to provide a message. A song about an argument with a friend may be best left as a song about an argument with a friend. Attempts to force resolutions, especially spiritual resolutions, can seem unnatural. Even life as experienced by a Christian isn't like that. We go to a wedding feast but no water is turned to wine. We go fishing but no one comes and points out the best place to fish.

If we are cautious about how and when we introduce God by name, his appearance will have an impact that it loses if scattered through almost everything we do. Some of the most powerful Christian work I have encountered has featured God as a powerful yet unnamed presence, and more powerful for being unnamed. Into this category I would put songs like Paul Stookey's "Hymn," written for a wedding service, and Bob Dylan's "Every Grain of Sand," which refers only to "the master's hand."

We needn't write only about the good and uplifting things of life. Christian painting doesn't have to be restricted to landscapes and portraits of puppy dogs. Christian music shouldn't feel compelled to offer comfort and sweet melodies. Christian novels shouldn't always be about bad people who convert or converted people who triumph over adversity. To portray the world as a rose garden can be as misleading as portraying it as a cesspool.

Any honest reflection on life will deal with imperfection. The difference in a Christian artist's work should be that the depraved will seem depraved, the ugly will seem ugly. Christians should be distinguished from those who suggest that depravity is normal or that evil is good. A Christian photographer would want to record beauty but would also want to draw attention to ugliness and brutality in a way that would remind us that these conditions are unnatural.

The southern novelist and short-story writer Flannery O'Connor was a brilliant exponent of the world as it is. Her fiction is full of grotesque characters and bizarre situations, but she argued that it was because of, rather than in spite of, her Christian beliefs that she wrote like this. She felt that knowing that perfection existed allowed her to see imperfection for what it really was.

> My own feeling is that writers who see by the light of their Christian faith will have, in these times, the sharpest eyes for the grotesque, for the perverse, and for the unacceptable. . . . Redemption is meaningless unless there is a cause for it in the actual life we live, and for the last few centuries there has been operating in our culture the secular belief that there is no such cause.[5]

Dualism has deep historic roots. Christianity (not the Bible) inherited it from the philosophy of Plato, but it was probably in existence long before him. Plato's belief was that the body and its desires are an encumbrance. Relief could only come at death when the body released the soul.

> I reckon we make the nearest approach to knowledge when we have the least possible intercourse or communion with the body, and are not surfeited with the bodily nature, but keep ourselves pure until the hour when God himself is pleased to release us and thus having got rid of the foolishness of the body we shall be pure and hold converse with the pure, and know of ourselves the clear light everywhere, which is no other than the light of truth.[6]

Paul, in his letters, refers to the battle between the "spirit" and the "flesh" which has often been interpreted as a conflict between a higher and lower nature with the Christian life being spent taming physical desires so that spiritual desires can take over control. Not surprisingly, this view gave rise to complex techniques for beating the lower nature into submission: abstinence, fasting, monasticism, and even flagellation and mutilation.

Yet Paul was not a Platonist. In talking about the "flesh" and the "spirit" he was distinguishing between desires controlled by God and those that aren't. Paul recognized that most sins are initiated by an appeal to the senses. The original temptation was to Eve's sight and taste. But tongues and eyes are not bad things. When Paul talks about putting to death "the old self" he is not suggesting that we are to mortify our five senses but to ensure that they are controlled by a mind which is undergoing constant renewal.

People with renewed minds are not to approach life as if sensually numbed, as though they can't wait to escape into the next life. If anything they should approach it with new vigor and increased understanding. My experience of balanced Christians has been that they enjoy life so much more than the average person. Heaven to them doesn't mark a complete break with earthly experience but an intensification of all that is good about it with the addition of unimagined new dimensions.

Our supreme example is Jesus Christ. God came to earth in human form and yet didn't confine himself to what a religious Jew of the time would have considered to be the sacred area of life. He didn't sit in the temple or wear priestly clothing. He lived alongside ordinary people, went for walks, ate and drank with sinners, built furniture, slept, wept, relaxed, cared for his mother, sailed in boats, and attended social functions.

In fact, the criticism of the Pharisees and Sadducees was that he wasn't religious enough; he was too secular. But the lesson was that God wasn't interested only in the narrow sphere of religious experience. He was concerned with the totality of life and showed his approval by living it. Each time Christ performed a human activity, he was blessing it.

Art, it must be remembered, has intrinsic value. A Christian doctor doesn't normally feel the need to justify the medical profession even though it often provides little opportunity for presentations of the gospel. Medicine, we all realize, is on God's side simply by relieving pain, healing damaged bodies, fighting disease and extending lives. It is for life and against death. It is for preservation and against decay. It attempts to limit the effects of the Fall. Jesus practiced healing and not always, from what we can determine, in order that those that were healed would also be saved.

In a similar way, the arts can act on God's side by preserving beauty and drawing out the highest achievements capable by humans. The arts can help preserve and renew cultures and this is a good thing in itself. This must bring God pleasure. The arts can sharpen the vision, quicken the intellect, preserve the memory, activate the conscience, enhance the understanding and refresh the language. Poetry, for example, is a useful antidote for the poison of sloganeering, spin and double talk. It helps words retain their meaning because it acknowledges that corrupt language results in corrupt thinking. If the best words can no longer be said, the best ideas can no longer be thought. "If a nation's literature declines," said Ezra Pound, "the nation atrophies and decays."

The visual arts help us to see with greater clarity. They draw our attention to overlooked details. They restore our sense of amazement. Dance resensitizes us to the grace of movement. Fiction provides us with unique access to other minds, cultures and periods of history. Music supplies us with hints of the transcendent. It is surely significant that art suffers when cultures decline. The Old Testament often gives us the haunting image of the cessation of music and singing when a civilization crumbles.

Sometimes doctors choose to become missionary doctors, but not usually because they feel that medicine is only justified when harnessed to a gospel program. Similarly, there are many artists who choose to create obviously religious art, and hopefully they too aren't doing so because they feel that their work would otherwise be worthless. Just as some people would rather compose cantatas than light orchestral pieces, they would rather paint biblical scenes than self-portraits. The church requires their talent. We cannot criticize the standard of worship songs, Sunday school literature or youth fellowship drama if we don't encourage writers and artists to do their best in these areas.

The problem comes when artists who could be contributing to the discussion taking place in the mainstream arts are hidden away in the church, and artists who should be sticking to the church are deluded into thinking that they are going to transform contemporary culture. I have known people who thought they were Christian Bruce Springsteens but were in fact much better suited to be worship leaders and writers of contemporary hymns. At the same time, I've known singers and songwriters who I thought could have competed with the giants of rock who have fallen back on the comfort zone of the Christian art and entertainment scene.

Then there are some artists, not too many, who manage to create overt Christian art that appeals outside of the church. Gerard Manley Hopkins did so with his poetry and Thomas Merton with his essays, journals and spiritual books. John Tavener is one of the most celebrated classical composers in the world today, and almost all of his work is unapologetically inspired by his exploration of Christian thought through the Greek Orthodox Church. R. S. Thomas, one of the greatest Welsh poets of the twentieth century (he died in September 2000), was also a clergyman, and his poetry was dominated by his personal wrestling with God. Howard Finster, the folk artist from Alabama whose work has decorated the covers of albums by REM and Talking Heads, emblazons his work with Bible texts and spiritual advice.

Contemporary artists not working within a church culture who make spiritual experience the dominant theme of their work are extremely rare. They are usually tenacious and slightly eccentric. Because there is no overlap of experience with the secular mind, what they do has to succeed because it is so powerful that even those unbelievers are overwhelmed. A writer in the *London Times*, commenting on Tavener's work recently, wrote, "One may dissent from Tavener's theology and dislike its emotive centrality in his work, but there is always his formal sense to consider. Despite his belief that his religious music must be as limpid and ego-less as an Eden stream, he never lets go of a certain artistic cunning." When the rock critic Greil Marcus reviewed *Belle*, an album by the singer turned preacher Al Green, he remarked that the record carried "a sense of liberation and purpose deep enough to make the sinner envy the saved."

In one of the last interviews he gave, R. S. Thomas was musing on one of the problems that concerns every artist who is a Christian. How do we talk about God in a godless world? How can we discuss the basics of Christian theology when the words and symbols traditionally used to do so have lost their currency? For the answers to such questions, we should turn to the Bible.

five

the bible

It's often assumed that the Bible has nothing to say about the arts. After all, most of it was written from within a religious culture in which there was no secular arts establishment and no concept of art as evangelism. The art referred to in the Bible was made by and for believers in God.

Additionally, the art forms that dominate our culture are comparatively recent. The Bible authors had experience of music and storytelling but not of rock, film or the novel. The fact that David danced before the Lord doesn't help us very much in choreographing contemporary physical theater; the details of tabernacle design and ark construction are not a sufficient basis for twenty-first century architecture.

What the Bible does give us is actually more substantial than a detailed guide. It gives us basic doctrines that can be applied to any art form in any age, and it gives us the wonderful example of itself. The Bible is a work of art that not only has survived over the centuries but has inspired artists in every generation since it came into being.

The doctrines of creation, fall and redemption are foundational to any Christian understanding. If we get any of these three wrong, our theology, and therefore our art, will be warped.

The doctrine of creation teaches us that God made human beings in his image for the purpose of serving him in love and looking after the things he made. Creativity is part of that inherited image because God is a designer and maker. Our desire to create, our ability to make concepts tangible and our pleasure in making are all reflections of God's original "let there be" and "it was good."

This means that creativity is not merely permissible, it is essential. It is what God wants. To express ourselves in art is to experience more fully the richness of being human. Animals may make primitive tools, be taught to recognize sounds and instinctively make such complexly designed habitats as a web or a honeycomb, but only humans make art.

The first tasks given to Adam were cultural. He had to work and take care of his environment, and he was given a responsibility for building language. During the naming of the animals we are told that God was interested "to see what he would name them" (Genesis 2:19) indicating that God derived pleasure from Adam's creative acts. This activity of naming, buried as it might be in the whole sweep of Scripture, is significant because a similar impulse is felt by artists. In our era biologists and zoologists actually do the naming of animals, but artists give names to moods, feelings, concepts and insights—and the "names" aren't always in words. "To evoke in oneself a feeling one has experienced," wrote Tolstoy about the creating of art, "and having evoked it in oneself, then by means of movement, line, colors, sounds or forms expressed in words so to transmit that feeling that others experience the same feeling—that is the activity of art."[1]

In this context it's interesting to note that Shakespeare invented over two thousand words during the writing of his poems and plays, many of which are still in use. He brilliantly captured the process of artistic creation in the voice of Theseus in "A Midsummer Night's Dream":

The poet's eye, in a fine frenzy rolling,
Doth glance from heaven to earth, from earth to heaven;
And as imagination bodies forth
The form of things unknown, the poet's pen
Turns them into shapes, and gives to airy nothing
A local habitation and a name.

The entry of sin in the world didn't extinguish creativity or relieve us of the responsibility of working, caring and naming. Noah built an ark; Jacob designed and made a beautiful coat for his son Joseph. To create the splendor of the tabernacle God prepared a craftsman named Bezalel: "I have filled him with the spirit of God, with skill, ability and knowledge in all kinds of crafts—to make artistic designs for work in gold, silver and bronze, to cut and set stones, to work in wood, and to engage in all kids of craftsmanship" (Exodus 31:2-5).

Music is also part of our creative heritage from God. Jubal, an early descendant of Adam, invented and played musical instruments, becoming "the father of all who play the harp and flute" (Genesis 4:21). Moses composed and sang a song; Miriam danced. Later on in the Old Testament we read of music, song, poetry and dance being used in worship, which suggests that although God is responsive to the most inarticulate groan (as Paul indicates), he expects us to be expressive and creative in our praise. There is something in him that warms to the sight of a thousand people dancing and banging tambourines, to the thoughts of the diligent psalmist, to the sound of a mass choir.

Yet a doctrine of creation alone is insufficient. It doesn't explain the presence of evil in the world or why there is a gap between the way we think we should behave and the way we actually behave. A doctrine of creation alone leads us to think that our problems are merely ones of perception or bad habits, and that if we were able to raise our consciousnesses or get our lives in order we could reestablish our union with God.

The doctrine of the Fall tells us that the wrong in the world stems from an original rebellion against God and that all acts of sin are a reflection of that rebellion. This doesn't mean that the world is as bad as it can be, but it does mean that it isn't as good as it once was. Everything, including our greatest art, is marred. The fact of sinful nature means that creativity can be used against God. Like the rain, the gifts of the artist are distributed to both the godly and the ungodly. Many great artists have used their skills to deny the existence of God and to mock the Christian church.

Artists, even those who are Christian, are fallen people observing a fallen world. Because the world is fallen we have to take notice of its brokenness and acknowledge it in our work. Because we ourselves are fallen we have to monitor our perceptions, because we know that they can be distorted by sin. We should hesitate before calling anything we do Christian art because we don't know how much of our own pride, selfishness or ignorance has polluted our vision.

There is a mood around today, even among Christians, that bristles at the mention of the Fall. Such an idea seems too negative. Why can't we talk only of the wonders of creation and the glory of humanity? Surely doing this would help bring about a more positive world! For example, an evangelical arts magazine favorably reviewed a book where the author "interprets the Fall not as a premeditated choice of evil, but as an allegory of the inevitable alienation experienced by humans upon evolving beyond the threshold of self-knowledge. The Fall is therefore a necessary step in the evolution of the cosmos."

These arguments can sound persuasive to artists, particularly to those who have suffered under expressions of Christianity where the joyous and creative has been squashed and where the extent of sin has been exaggerated. Matthew Fox, the Dominican priest and promoter of creation spirituality who was expelled from the order in 1993 for departing from church teaching and associating with witches, in his book *Original Blessing* condemns what he calls "fall/redemption spirituality" for "not teaching believers about the New

Creation or creativity, about justice-making and social transformation, or about Eros, play, pleasure and the God of delight."[3]

But the way out of any distorted form of Christianity is not by abandoning the doctrine of the Fall or by softening the momentousness of the historical act by relegating it to the level of allegory. The solution is to constantly hold the Fall in balance with the doctrine of creation. The world is neither so full of evil that we can't enjoy it nor so full of goodness that we can abandon ourselves to it. When we see something beautiful there is always the qualifying thought that it is tarnished. When we see something ugly, there is always the qualifying thought that there is something of the Creator hidden there.

The doctrines of creation and fall, taken alone, are also insufficient. They would let us know only that God made a good world and something went wrong. We wouldn't know whether God maintains an interest or whether he has any plans to restore his creation.

The doctrine of redemption, the idea that God has initiated a rescue plan, completes the picture. The decisive action has been taken, the results are already in motion, and there is a new heaven and a new earth to come. A moral standard does exist in the universe, and any sin not already punished on the cross will be dealt with on Judgment Day.

While we cannot perfect the world through urging people to live better lives, it is our duty as Christians to restrain evil and encourage good. In the Sermon on the Mount, Jesus referred to his followers as "salt of the earth" and "light of the world" (Matthew 5:13, 14). These images are helpful in allowing us to see what part our art can play in the overall plan of redemption.

Jesus wasn't offering an option—you can be salt or, if you're really keen, you can be light. He was saying that the faithful Christian will automatically perform both functions. The salt is an image of a preservative. In the absence of refrigeration it was what his audience put on their fish and meat. It didn't bring life to the flesh but it slowed down the process of decay. The light is an image of guidance and revelation. With a candle or lamp you could know where you were and could explore without being hampered.

Because of redemption, our art can be both salt and light. It can hinder the spread of evil, and it can offer guidance. The lamp in Jesus' illustration was put on a stand, suggesting that we should be where those in need of illumination are most likely to see us. The result was that it "gives light to everyone in the house" (Matthew 5:15). Our light is not for the benefit of those who already have light.

These are the doctrines that should inform the work of the artist who is a Christian. But beyond that we will find inspiration in the Bible documents themselves—not just in what is said but in how the human creators approach their subjects and the techniques they use to make the truth vivid.

Anyone who has grown up with a knowledge of the Bible is well schooled in the use of typology and metaphor. Before ever learning what a type is we know that the blood daubed on the lintels of the Jewish homes at the time of the Passover foreshadowed the blood of Christ; the ark that survived the flood spoke of the future intervention of Christ as Savior.

It's impossible to read the Gospels or the letters of Paul without accustoming ourselves to such metaphors as "the bride of Christ," "the old self," "born again," "the Word," "in Adam" and "a thorn in the flesh." We accept quite naturally that Jesus can be both a shepherd and a lamb, a servant and a king, the seed and the vine.

Even the most familiar words of Jesus are made memorable by what we would now refer to as literary techniques. The truths he was communicating were so vast that they couldn't be contained in plain speech. In the Sermon on the Mount he used aphorism ("Where your treasure is, there your heart will be also," Matthew 6:21), anaphora (the repetition of "Blessed are," Matthew 5:3-11), metaphor ("You are the salt of the earth," Matthew 5:13), personification ("Tomorrow will worry about itself," Matthew 6:34), analogy ("Every tree that does not bear good fruit is cut down and thrown into the fire. Thus, by their fruit you will recognize them," Matthew

7:19-20) and hyperbole ("You hypocrite, first take the plank out of your own eye," Matthew 7:5).

In his storytelling—forty parables are recorded in the Gospels—he used allegory to make spiritual points and set them in the familiar landscape of seeds, birds, rocks, weeds, fish, vineyards, corn, watchtowers and oil lamps. When questioned by those who doubted him he often answered ambiguously. When Nicodemus flattered him about his miracles he responded with "I tell you the truth, unless a man is born again, he cannot see the kingdom of God" (John 3:3). When questioned about the legitimacy of Roman taxes he said, "Give to Caesar what is Caesar's, and to God what is God's" (Matthew 22:21). When accused by Pilate he stayed silent.

Artists have always been particularly attracted to the books of poetry, wisdom and prophecy in the Bible because there they meet people of like mind, people who approached truth from oblique angles and who were willing to confront their failure and despair as well as their triumphs and joys.

David and his fellow psalmists are a role model for poets. It's not just the beauty of the words and the phrases that have become part of our language but the remarkable honesty of the writers as they report back on the vicissitudes of the spiritual life. To read one psalm after another is to be taken on a roller-coaster ride that repeatedly switches from glory to gloom and back again.

"O LORD, do not rebuke me" (Psalm 6) is followed by "O LORD my God, I take refuge in you" (Psalm 7), which in turn leads to "O LORD, our Lord, how majestic is your name" (Psalm 8) and then "I will praise you, O LORD, with all my heart" (Psalm 9). Just as you think everything is harmonious there is, "Why, O LORD, do you stand far off?" (Psalm 10). They convince because they feel like real life. The psalms that comfort are very often the ones that show that even a "man after God's own heart" like David could get mad with God and feel let down.

The psalms give voice to our grievances and objections. No book in the Bible has a more extensive use of the adverbs *why* or *how:*

Why does God hide himself from us? Why am I so cast down? Why do the nations fight? Why do the wicked prosper while the godly suffer? How long will this go on? Bono, lead singer of the rock group U2, sees these psalmists as blues singers "shouting at God."[4]

They also record the lowest of times in unflinching detail: rejection, unanswered prayer, remorse, sickness, pain, oppression, persecution. "I am worn out from groaning; all night long I flood my bed with weeping and drench my couch with tears" (Psalm 6:6). "I know my transgressions, and my sin is always before me" (Psalm 51:3).

The psalms encourage the Christian to be as honest about the questions as the answers, as revealing about the times when God seems absent as the times when his presence is overwhelming. They show how it is possible to create works expressing faith that overlap with the experience of the unbeliever.

In even greater detail Ecclesiastes portrays a world that the person of little or no faith would recognize. It's a world where God exists but apparently has no current interest in his creation. The writer considers that there is no ultimate meaning and so, through a series of experiments, tries to create enough purpose to make life worth living. He improves his understanding (wisdom, knowledge), blots out his depression (madness, folly, laughter, wine) and builds alternative worlds (power, property, sex, wealth).

Eleven of the book's twelve chapters are devoted to his doomed search to make existence tolerable. God is remote, uninvolved and offers no purpose or salvation. "God is in heaven and you are on earth, so let your words be few" (Ecclesiastes 5:2). It's only in the final chapter that hope is offered: "Fear God and keep his commandments, for this is the whole duty of man" (Ecclesiastes 12:1).

When I first read Ecclesiastes it seemed to me to be the most contemporary sounding book in the Bible. It appeared to be coming from the same place as Samuel Beckett's play *Waiting for Godot*,[5] the Beatles' song "Nowhere Man" (1965), J. D. Salinger's novel *The Catcher in the Rye*[6] or the paintings of Francis Bacon. The writer dared to question the significance of life if God could be presumed absent, if there was creation and fall but no redemption.

For Christians this is a fruitful but largely unexplored area. If secularism is a false view, why not imaginatively explore it to expose its weaknesses and inconsistencies? Sometimes an audience needs to be confronted with the bankruptcy of its own beliefs before it is willing to even consider an alternative. To employ some other words from Ecclesiastes, "There is a time to tear down and a time to build" (Ecclesiastes 3:3).

A Christian could, like the absurdist dramatists of the 1950s and 1960s, simply reveal the purposelessness of a world in which God is assumed to be dead. The secular mind frequently doesn't face up to the full implications of its beliefs; art can provide a timely shock that results in a reassessment. A Christian could also use satire to a similar effect, exposing the intellectual weakness of secularism.

The book of Proverbs illustrates how art can be used to spread wisdom. Christians can often be so preoccupied with salvation that they ignore the value of common sense. Although God is at the back of every saying in Proverbs—"the fear of the LORD is the beginning of wisdom" (Proverbs 9:10)—almost all of the advice given is without direct reference to God and is intended to be beneficial to anyone willing to listen.

Proverbs offers advice on how to have a good marriage, how to give generously, how to avoid bad company, how to be industrious, how to hold your tongue, how to be honest in business dealings. There is no suggestion that we'll be saved if we follow these instructions, but society, if it is to run smoothly, continually needs to be reminded of such basic wisdom. This is the salt that prevents decay.

The epigrammatic style of Proverbs is perfectly suited to its purpose. The sentences are so compact they are almost like advertising slogans. They hook into the consciousness and have a habit of remaining there for a lifetime. Who can forget "pride comes before a fall," an adaptation of Proverbs 11:2, or "stolen water tastes sweet," an adaptation of Proverbs 9:17? Our experience confirms their truth.

There is a need for wisdom in art. Shock, surprise, novelty and innovation help to grab attention but are not substantial in themselves. If we only confront or stun people it's as if we have tapped them on the shoulder or tugged on their coat, but when they've responded by turning around, we have had nothing of benefit to say to them.

The Song of Songs is a graphic love poem. Early church historian Jerome reported that Jews forbade it to be read to anyone under the age of thirty. Traditionally it has been seen as an allegory of the relationship between Christ and his chosen people with no attention paid to the human dimension. While it may have an allegorical level, commentators in the past have had to perform some amazing interpretive gymnastics to maintain that this is the only level. For example, Jamieson, Fausset and Brown in their nineteenth-century *Commentary on the Whole Bible*, understood "Your breasts are like two fawns, twins of a gazelle" (Song 7:3) to be a reference to faith and love.[7]

It seems to me that Jews in the Old Testament period would have taken it at face value as a poem that endorsed love between a man and a woman, and celebrated its physical expression. What stands out is the intense passion. The couple can't wait to be together. They admire each other's bodies. They kiss and embrace. All the senses are stimulated.

Writing about legitimate sexual expression in the current permissive climate can be difficult but, as Bono once said, "Why should we allow the pornographers a monopoly on sexuality?" If we never refer to our sexual feelings we can give the impression that salvation desexes us or that we identify sexual longing with original sin. Sex and sexuality are among the most discussed issues in the arts today.

It is a sensitive issue for the Christian. We don't want to invoke lust or betray confidences. We don't want to engage in "art as exorcism" exercises by unburdening our past histories and current fantasies. Nor do we want to promote the "sex as salvation" line that sees orgasmic excitement as union with God. But it would be good to counter the demonic lie that infidelity and fornication are exciting whereas commitment and marriage are boring.

One of the best examples I've come across in recent years is the song "Love Cocoon" recorded by The Vigilantes of Love, written by vocalist Bill Mallonee for his wife. It combines the language of the Song of Songs with the aggression of John Donne's Holy Sonnets:

> Honey, I wanna attack your flesh with glad abandon
> I wanna look for your fruits, I wanna put my hands on 'em

and ending four verses later with

> Some call it freedom, some call it shackled
> Honey, let's get together and build a tabernacle
> of holy flesh, holy mirth
> Let's take what's coming, enjoy every inch worth.[8]

If songwriters and poets are inspired by Psalms and the Song of Songs, dramatists are inspired by Job, which is like a play for six voices. The prologue shows God offering Job as an example of faithfulness and obedience and then Satan challenging this by saying that Job wouldn't be like this if he had everything taken away from him. God then allows Satan to test Job through a series of calamities.

The questions posed by the book of Job are still among the most frequently asked. If there is a God, why does he allow suffering? When things go wrong in our lives, is it always a direct result of our behavior? Job's faith is never extinguished, but he doesn't conceal his feeling of abandonment. "I cry to you O God, but you do not answer" he says (Job 30:20). "All was well with me, but he shattered me; he seized me by the neck and crushed me. He has made me his target" (Job 16:12).

A lot of art comes out of pain and so, not surprisingly, a lot of art deals with the problem of suffering. If we only have a doctrine of creation we have to accept that suffering is a part of what is. If, on the other hand, we have a doctrine of the Fall but nothing else, we can reject suffering as an abnormality, but we can't promise anything better. With a doctrine of redemption we can see how God allows suffering in his overall plan of healing and how death has been beaten.

The final type of Bible writing that inspires artists is prophecy. Today there is an expectation that art can be prophetic in both senses of the word: it can anticipate the future, and it can challenge society's morals. Because artists are not so bound to conventional patterns of thinking they tend to adopt today the lifestyles of tomorrow. The phrase *avant garde* literally means "vanguard," those who go ahead of the main party to check out the territory. Ezra Pound, himself part of the literary avant garde, who once boasted that "artists are the antennae of the race," observed that "artists and poets undoubtably get excited about things long before the general public."[9]

There is also an assumption that artists will tend to prick the pretensions of those in power, call attention to injustice and attack untested assumptions about behavior. Beat poet Allen Ginsberg consciously presented himself as a prophet, attacking American foreign policy during the 1960s in poetry that borrowed its style and imagery from Old Testament writers such as Jeremiah. During most of this time he even looked like the popular stereotype of a prophet—simple cotton clothing, a long dark beard and a musical instrument.

This conception of the artist as prophet is derived from the biblical model, but artists weren't viewed in this light until the Romantic period. The main reason for the change was the book *Lectures on the Sacred Poetry of the Hebrews* (1753) by the theologian Robert Lowth, which influenced poets such as William Blake. One of Lowth's conclusions was that the Hebrew word *Nabi*, translated as prophet in the King James Version, could equally well mean poet or musician.

> It is sufficiently evident that the prophetic office had a most strict connection with the poetic art. . . . They had one common name, one common origin, one common author, the Holy Spirit. Those in particular were called to the exercise of the prophetic office, who were previously conversant with the sacred poetry. It was equally part of their duty to compose verses for the service of the church, and to declare the oracles of God.[10]

Genuine prophets were people who passed the words of God on to the people. They expressed his feelings about particular behavior, predicted the results of obedience and disobedience, and foretold events in both the near and distant future. They were not always popular figures.

This is not the place for a debate about whether the gift of prophecy continues today. But the actions of the prophets do suggest possibilities to artists. Like artists, they appear to have existed on the margins of society. Perhaps by not being at the center of things they were able to keep a sharper perspective. There is also a close relationship between music and prophecy, almost as if the playing of music prepared the mind to be receptive to God's message. The "company of prophets" who meet Saul at Gibeah are playing lyres, tambourines, flutes and harps (1 Samuel 10:5).

In the voices of the prophets we can hear an anger and condemnation which reminds us of the protest music of the 1960s, the punk rock of the 1970s and the rap in the 1990s. This music forced society to face up to unpleasant facts about its behavior. British philosopher and historian of ideas R. G. Collingwood, in his *Essays in the Philosophy of Art*, says, "The artist must prophesy not in the sense that he foretells things to come, but in the sense that he tells his audience, at the risk of their displeasure, the secrets of their own hearts."[11]

Besides speaking, singing and playing musical instruments the prophets often performed bizarre acts which were designed to provoke and shock. Ezekiel lay on his side for a year. Another time he shaved his head. Jeremiah hid his underwear in a crevice until it rotted and then displayed it as an illustration of how God saw the Israel's pride. Ahijah tore his cloak into twelve pieces. Hosea married an adulteress to demonstrate how God viewed the unfaithfulness of the chosen people.

These acts remind us of some of the more controversial conceptual and performance art of our own day. We might think of Damien Hirst's decaying cow's head in a glass case titled *A Thousand Years*

(1990) or Joseph Beuys's *How to Explain Pictures to a Dead Hare* (1965), in which he stood for three hours with his head smeared with honey muttering to an animal corpse that he cradled in his arms. Like the acts of the prophets, these works puzzle, provoke and prompt questions.

It might surprise us that some of the most controversial art today has biblical precedents, but that's the kind of book the Bible is. It is the living Word, and the exciting thing is that although God, and therefore his truth, remains unchangeable, the Bible yields new insight to every believer and every generation. It is when we treat it as the mummified Word of God that we find ourselves stuck with only one cultural expression of our faith, usually one from at least a century ago.

What we need to do is dig deep and develop fresh understandings to prepare us for our art and our age. The same book that fired the imaginations of Milton and Bunyan in the seventeenth century can open up new possibilities for us in the twenty-first century.

the mind

f, as I have suggested, the art made by Christians need not be overtly religious and doesn't have to justify itself by "winning the world for Christ," then what is there to distinguish it from any other art? The key comes from using what Harry Blamires calls "the Christian mind."[1] A person begins to look at the world in a different way after conversion, and this affects everything.

This new way of seeing comes partly through biblical revelation. The convert learns new truths that could never have been discovered through reason alone. But the Christian mind isn't created entirely through theology. There is the presence of the Holy Spirit who generates new attitudes that result in new forms of behavior. As the Lord says to Ezekiel, "I will put my Spirit in you and move you to follow my decrees and be careful to keep my laws" (Ezekiel 36:27). The apostle Paul refers to the result of this as the "fruit of the Spirit."

Some converts, particularly those who've been brought from deep despair, are more aware than others of the stark contrast between the old and new ways of perception. They not only see God in a different way but they see themselves, others and nature in a different way. Many written testimonies speak of people finding their nature transformed after conversion as everything takes on a fresh significance. The words of the old hymn "I Am His and He Is Mine" capture this:

> Heaven above is softer blue
> Earth around is sweeter green,
> Something lives in every hue
> Christless eyes have never seen.[2]

Reality as viewed by a Christian is different from reality seen through secular eyes. The fact that we are aware of an eternity ahead and spiritual realms around us alters our perspective on everything else. We have a different view of good and evil. We have a different view of truth. We have a different view of the person. As Blamires points out:

> To think secularly is to think within a frame of reference bounded by the limits of our life on earth: it is to keep one's calculations rooted in this-worldly criteria. To think Christianly is to accept all things with the mind as related, directly or indirectly, to man's eternal destiny as the redeemed and chosen child of God.[3]

Again and again in the New Testament nonbelievers are described as having hearts that are "blinded" and conversion is likened to having sight restored. This is dramatically illustrated in the conversion of Paul who is literally blinded by a light on the road to Damascus so that when he receives the Holy Spirit at the laying of hands by Ananias "something like scales" fell from his eyes, and he immediately went to be baptized.

This is not to say that when we become Christians we see everything clearly, but I think it emphasizes that we see things with fresh sight. Owen Chadwick, in his book *A History of Christianity*, makes the interesting observation that the earliest art known to have been made by Christians, found on the walls of the catacombs of Rome, is characterized by a lack of anxiety in the faces of those approaching death. This might seem a small thing, but it is indicative of a whole new attitude that was introduced after the death and resurrection of Christ. "The images are serene, not sad, confident in life after death, and full of peace," writes Chadwick.[4]

Yet the renewed mind is not just obvious in its response to such big issues as death but in its response to the minutiae of life. We feel differently about trees, leaves, rain, bad housing, animals, food, money, sex, social standing, leisure, poverty. One of the effects of conversion is that our priorities are shaken up. We understand for the first time the truth of such paradoxes as "the first shall be last" and "whoever loses his life for my sake will find it." We understand how the rich can be poor and the poor can be rich.

Christians develop a view of the world where all of creation points to God. Jesus taught that in caring for the sick, imprisoned and starving we are caring for him. The writer of Hebrews says that we should entertain strangers "for by so doing some people have entertained angels without knowing it" (13:2). Paul, in the first chapter of Romans, points out that God's "invisible qualities" are made known to us through nature (Romans 1:20). In the words of the poet Gerard Manley Hopkins, "The world is charged with the grandeur of God."[5]

I have found it helpful to think of what the Christian might do in art in terms of five concentric circles. The gospel of death and resurrection is at the center. It affects everything else, and it is so precious and yet so divisive that we need to approach it cautiously. I am not going back on what I have already said about the art of the Christian not needing to be explicitly religious, but I think that Christians naturally feel compelled to say something about what they believe holds the key to the human problem.

But there are some artists who may not be called to go that far in their art. It may be that their particular art form wasn't built to explore such grand subjects. If someone was a burlesque entertainer, for example, it wouldn't be appropriate to try and create an act that dealt with sin and redemption. It may be possible to do it, but the result of combining a form created to deal with the light-hearted aspects of life with the greatest issues humankind has ever dealt with is likely to be unrewarding. Similarly, certain forms of pop music can't easily deal with big themes without descending into bathos.

With each art form and each genre within each art form we must always ask ourselves what would be appropriate. We don't have to be confined by what has gone before, because all breakthroughs in art have come about because someone attempted what was previously thought impossible, but we do have to consider how great a leap we might make without appearing ridiculous.

Some artists just wouldn't be good at it, just as some church deacons would make bad evangelists. It takes a different sort of talent to sensitively explore, in art, the issues surrounding the cross. If someone does it enthusiastically but badly, it can have an adverse effect. The cross itself is off-putting enough to the secular mind without having it communicated through bad art.

Also, as I have already alluded to, I have at all times been aware of those artists who don't determine the point of view of the art that they are contriburing. I am thinking of the drummer in the band who has no hand in the writing of the songs, the actor who isn't at liberty to alter the screenplay, the musician who faithfully follows the notes written by the composer, the dancer who obeys the instructions of the choreographer.

I am fortunate because writing is inseparable from a point of view. You can't write and not have a point of view. But there are many fellow artists whose primary concern is getting it right rather than saying something. They are learning lines, practicing chords, rehearsing movements. The issues they face are quite different from mine. Should they act in a film that has a nihilistic point of view? Should they portray adultery or fornication? Should they perform on Sundays?

I hope that the circles I'll describe here will be helpful even to these people because, as will be shown, work created by those who are nonbelievers can be consistent with a gospel outlook without having to deal with the heart of the gospel.

In my set of circles the outer ring is made up of art that doesn't suggest an obvious worldview, particularly if it's experienced out of the context of the rest of the artist's work. It could be someone playing bassoon in a school orchestra or dancing in a chorus line. It could be a nonsense song written for children, a portrait painting of a neighbor or a sculpture made out of an interesting piece of driftwood.

Of course, we may be able to detect a different slant; we may think that we can hear the accent of Jesus, but it is not overt. In the case of nonsense songs, we may point out that nonsense writing, by its very nature, reinforces logic, sense and order, but usually this sort of work is carried out in the spirit of play with no thought of any higher meaning.

This sort of art is justified by the things God himself made. Presumably marine ecology would be a simple science if all fish had been made in one color and one design, but God, as I have already pointed out, likes to experiment, embellish and impress. The different shapes and shades of leaves, the textures and smells of wood— all point to a God who loves design for its own sake. They are unsigned pieces of handiwork that give us insight into his character but tell us no more than that. They were made in a spirit of sheer delight, and the fact that we do things in the same spirit should not surprise us. God could, of course, have left written messages all over creation, but he didn't.

Should this art at least be functional? Shouldn't it answer some need? Not necessarily. Some of nature provides food, plays its part in the carbon cycle and gives us delight, but a lot of it is hidden away. Most of nature, including almost everything beneath the sea, is known only to God.

The next circle contains work that is an expression of our Christian faith because it dignifies human life and introduces a sense of awe. Art can have an invigorating effect on people by reminding them of the wonder of being alive. It doesn't even need to put it into words. It can be the sound of a jazz saxophone or the sight of a dancer, but inside we feel ourselves welling up because it is awakening our senses. This, in turn, can begin a process of questioning: Why is it so wonderful to be alive? What is the source of this wonder?

Many people are involved in working with art because they want to expand the quality of people's lives. Children whose lives have been blighted by war, famine or abuse are quite often reawakened by music, dance, poetry, painting and drama. Their senses are engaged. Their experience is enlarged. Their damaged "Godlikeness" is allowed to reemerge, and often for the first time, they feel the wonder of being human.

My experience of reading poetry to these children has shown that words, images and symbols can often penetrate their apparently closed worlds. Those who can barely speak begin to show signs of joy and appreciation. It's not too presumptuous to say that God uses art in the process of healing these lives.

The psalmist David said of himself that he was "fearfully and wonderfully made" (Psalm 138:14), and the art made by Christians should reflect this view of humanity. There is a trend in contemporary art to reduce humans and strip them of their dignity. There is the idea that we are nothing more than meat and body fluids, and some artists have become obsessed with squalor, degradation and decay.

But an artist who is a Christian can never portray people as such. People may commit such horrendous sins that they lose their own sense of dignity, but they never lose their dignity before God. They are still fearfully and wonderfully made, and the Christian eye will see beyond the damage and the workings of sin. The Catholic painter Georges Rouault, like many of his contemporaries, painted prostitutes, but the art critic Louis Vauxcelles noticed the difference: "Unlike Lautrec," he wrote, "when he (Rouault) paints a prostitute there is no cruel pleasure in seeing vice exalted by a creature. He suffers and he weeps."[6]

Just as art can show disrespect for humans in the way it portrays them, it can show disrespect for them in the way it treats them as consumers. It can cynically exploit the public need for transcendent experience. I was struck by an account of unemployed British youth written by journalist Jeremy Seabrook. In one of the encounters described in his book *Unemployment* he meets a group of boys in the northeast of England, and they begin discussing serious issues. The discussion rapidly moved into talk of car crashes, alien abductions, cannibalism and corpses. Seabrook concludes that their natural curiosity about life, death and other realms had been distorted.

> Somehow all the spiritual and moral questions which they asked at the beginning became locked into images of violence and horror which they have absorbed from TV and films. The most real and perplexing spiritual experiences become tangled. They can't leave the earth except in metaphors about man-made robots, journeys into space, beings from other worlds. The materialism of their lives holds captive even the capacity for spiritual experience; minds and spirits shackled, tethered to all those industries that exploit the credulity and awe. All the search and questing, their sense of wonder at human mortality, is diverted into channels that will make money for others.[7]

The third ring contains those things that carry an imprint of clear Bible teaching but which we know are not uniquely Christian. For example, we might make art that calls for peace, love, forgiveness or reconciliation, and we may be compelled to do so because of our faith, but these values are not exclusive to Christianity or even to religion. Some of the best-known art made in the cause of truth, peace and equality has been made by atheists.

There are certain teachings in the Bible the majority of people in the liberal-minded West would assent to, although they may quibble about the precise application. Most people are keen to support the principles of justice and of caring for the weak and marginalized. They think that a lot of what Jesus said in the Sermon on the Mount about comforting the grieving and blessing the peacemakers is pretty sound.

That these are biblical principles is a good enough reason for us to embrace them in our art. Because they are also values that are widely held today, they can form a useful bridge between the believing art community and an unbelieving audience. Rock acts like Bruce Cockburn would have had considerably more difficulty being accepted if their work didn't have a dimension of social concern that struck a chord. What such artists have to say about faith then becomes more interesting to a general audience because they can see that it has not produced piety alone but a social application that they approve of.

It is not Christian to make art that assumes that the world is unblemished. More than any other group of people we should be aware of the effect of evil and be ready to draw people's attention to it. "Having nothing to do with the fruitless deeds of darkness," writes Paul, " but rather expose them" (Ephesians 5:11). This can mean, on the one hand, using our art to point out structural evil—human rights violations, unjust political systems, exploitation of the poor and so on—and on the other hand admitting our own personal sinfulness.

Admission of personal sin has to be treated carefully because we live in a climate of exposure. Artists are routinely commended for being "daring," "honest," "frank" and "disturbing" by admitting to base desires. The American artist Jeff Koons shared the intimacies of his sexual relationship with Italian porn star Cicciolina. The British artist Tracey Emin scheduled an exhibit to feature the soiled and unmade bed on which she had contemplated suicide.

But the attitude behind such gut spilling is not one of remorse and shame but of brazenness. The sin, in their view, would be to hold back, and the virtue is in telling all. The Christian is bound by some important considerations. There is a responsibility not to use examples of our vileness as entertainment. "For it is shameful even to mention what the disobedient do in secret" (Ephesians 5:12). We must put the needs of others before our own: "Nobody should seek his own good, but the good of others" (1 Corinthians 10:24).

I sometimes hear Christians justify mentioning their weaknesses in their art because "I'm a sinner like everyone else." That is just not true. The Christian isn't a sinner like everyone else because a Christian is a forgiven sinner, and this alters his or her whole relationship to sin. Many nonbelievers see sin, as defined in the Bible, as their key to liberation, just as Adam and Eve saw rebellion against God as the gateway to unimaginable freedom. For a Christian, sin should be seen as the precise opposite. It feels like freedom often, yes, but it is in fact imprisonment.

T. Bone Burnett skillfully tackles this balance between admission of guilt and appropriate remorse in such songs as "The Criminal Under My Hat" and "Shut It Tight." In the latter song he begins:

> I find it hard sometimes to say the way that I feel
> I do the very things I hate to do

In the second verse he continues:

> I stumble like a drunk along this crazy path I walk
> I have a hundred thousand questions too
> I'll go to any length to prove that nothing is my fault
> Then later on I will deny the proof.

The fourth circle in gets closer to the heart of the gospel. The issues here are inspired by some of the Bible's primary theological themes. We might create art that draws its inspiration from the teachings of original sin, human moral freedom and the spiritual realm. But these, too, are themes that have been tackled by followers of other religions and those of no religion at all. One of the best-known novels carrying a thesis of original sin is William Golding's *Lord of the Flies,* where a group of schoolboys traveling abroad crash on a deserted island. The question that the novel posits is, will these boys, who symbolize innocence, be able to start afresh and build a community free from corruption? "The theme," says Golding, "is an attempt to trace the defects of society back to the defects of human nature."[8]

Anthony Burgess's 1962 novel *A Clockwork Orange*[9] (later made into a movie by Stanley Kubrick) explores the issue of behavioral science. If it were possible to reprogram a violent psychopath through aversion therapy, would it be moral to use it? Or is it more moral to allow people to choose their behavior even when that behavior is wrong? The novel was, according to Burgess, "built on the theme of man's free will, the existence of good and evil and the necessity of choice."

Even art about the spiritual world is not the exclusive preserve of the Christian artist. There are many contemporary artists who will gladly talk about the reality of "other planes" or the "bankruptcy of materialism." Few popular musicians have done more to put spirituality on the agenda than Van Morrison, although he adheres to no religion in particular. Albums like *Into the Music, Beautiful Vision, Inarticulate Speech of the Heart* and *A Sense of Wonder* are based on the premise that the seen world is surrounded by the unseen world of the spirit. In his work Morrison has explored the idea of being able to connect with that world through ecstatic experience.

It is in the center circle that the unique Christian gospel lies. Deists can talk about a creator God, Jews can talk about the importance of the law, Muslims can talk about obedience, atheists can talk about human dignity, New Agers can talk about spirituality. But only a Christian can talk, with personal conviction, of the life, miracles, substitutionary death, resurrection and ascension of Jesus. Only the Christian can talk about the need for repentance, faith and discipleship.

At the heart of this final circle stands the cross. It is the cross that makes sense of all the other issues for us. If we are Christians, it is surely the most important thing in our lives. It is relevant to artists because artists use their art to make sense of the world. Their art is both their tool of discovery and their means of transmitting their findings back to others. Many artists eventually find a system of thought or a way of life which they think offers solutions, and they then feel an obligation to share this knowledge. This makes sense. Why deal with individual peripheral problems if you feel that these things would sort themselves out naturally if the bigger problem was tackled?

For the poet Allen Ginsberg, for instance, the solution lay in expanding the consciousness, either though drugs like mescaline or through mystical experience. He believed that armed conflict, prejudice, ecological disaster, fear of death—all could be overcome if people were to achieve this mystical consciousness. Not everything he wrote was directly about this, but it lurked behind everything. It shaped the causes he got involved in, it runs through his collected essays, it was part of his daily practice and is a major theme in his diaries.

For the Christian the cross is the event in which everything finds its resolution. We deal with fears, hunger, wars, injustice, alienation and other problems in the short term with consolation, food, diplomacy, campaigns and friendship, but we know that the human condition can only ultimately be healed through the effects of what was achieved on the cross.

Yet the cross has been the subject of so much art throughout history. How can we hope to incorporate it into art that will disturb and challenge our culture as it should? It is relatively easy to make art of the cross that people simply recognize and then categorize, as in "Oh, there is a nice religious painting. That is from the Christian tradition." Hardened sinners can have great affection for hymns and pagans can enjoy gospel records because they are already inoculated with the phrases of "old time religion." The challenge is to present it in such a way that people become aware that this has a direct bearing on them.

I have found the cross hard to translate into art because it has been done so many times. How do we look at it in another way? How do we make these familiar things (the cross, thorns, nails, blood) seem unfamiliar and the unfamiliar things (atonement, sacrifice) seem familiar? How can we "survey the wonderful cross" and yet remove it from the pages of those musty old hymnals and set it, as it were, on the front page of the *New York Times*?

The unbelieving world can be interested in controversial art about the cross if it is controversial in a conventional way. This usually means taking the facts as believed by the church for centuries and messing with them. So Christ becomes a crucified woman, a self-deluded hippie with a band of acolytes or a practicing homosexual. Or the cross is taken and immersed in urine, broken into the shape of a swastika or turned upside down.

None of this is what is meant by the phrase "the offense of the cross." What offends in these cases is the disregard for theology, and the only ones likely to be offended, other than God, are Christians. The true "offense of the cross" is the offense to our pride when we are told that we are sinners in need of salvation and that salvation comes not through our own efforts but through an unattractive looking first-century execution.

The cross presents the artist with difficulties because although it contains complexity, and we never exhaust its marvels or comprehend the depth of its truths, it is unambiguous. Christ didn't die to teach us lessons about bravery or to encourage us when we face difficulties. He died because that was the penalty demanded by God for sin. Few people would condemn us for making art about the glories of creation or the benefits of forgiveness. Even talking about God can be quite acceptable. There is often very little content to God. He could be your God, my God or anybody's God. But Jesus brings definition, and the cross brings even more definition. The Word is one thing. The Word become flesh is another.

The cross is also hard to introduce because we know we are entering an area where there is little common ground between artist and audience (assuming that the artist is a Christian and the intended audience is largely not). If it is put explicitly, it will only make complete sense to someone whose eyes are already opened or someone whose eyes are at the point of being opened.

If I were to stand up in a New York poetry slam and deliver a poem about love, I could feel reasonably sure that the audience would relate to what I was saying because of their own experiences of love. Similarly, if I read a poem about the delights of nature, the awfulness of betrayal or the horrors of war, I would expect to find resonance in their own histories. But what response would I get if I read a poem about the death of Christ?

People might snicker. They might feel uncomfortable. In some art circles religion, especially Christianity, is a matter for laughs. I could get shouted at. There are some who see Christianity as the cause of all kinds of repression. Most likely I would be faced with bemusement. Is he serious? Is he being ironic? Is he writing something in homage to Milton or Dante?

We don't arrive at the truths of the cross through a normal process of reasoning. It is possible to come to the idea of God after looking at creation and calculating that there must be a force behind it. We know that peace is better than war after we see the effects of violence. But the cross isn't a logical deduction, which is why the Greeks who "sought after wisdom" (1 Corinthians 1:22) thought it was so foolish. The facts of God and sin do not lead inexorably to the fact of a savior. God may, as some have suggested, have made the world, found it faulty and moved on to more improved creations elsewhere in the universe. The truth of the cross has to come through spiritual revelation.

It is easy to state the bare facts of the cross. The difficulty is to do it in a way that is consistent with the rest of our art and that engages our audience. It is easy to write a song that says "The savior of the world died on a tree/In order to save you and me" but how many people have their perceptions rattled by such language? Art should be helping us see things as if we had never seen them before. "We need to clean our windows," said writer J. R. R. Tolkien, "so that the things seen clearly may be freed from the drab blur of triteness or familiarity."[10]

It is by no means a new problem. David Lyle Jeffrey in his excellent study of Christian identity and literary culture, *People of the Book*,[11] shows how the anonymous author of the eighth-century poem "Dream of the Rood" faced similar issues. He wanted to write about the cross in a pagan culture that viewed a passive acceptance of death as disgraceful. He had to show that despite his meekness and mercy, Christ was fighting a heroic battle against death itself. The device the author used was to make the cross itself the narrator of the poem.

In more modern times painters, novelists and filmmakers have sought to rescue the cross from becoming a mere symbol by reasserting its shockingness. Christ on a first-century hilltop can seem quite beautiful, but Christ nailed to a garage door or crucified among pylons and satellite dishes is as unsettling an image as a gangland execution or a terrorist bombing.

The impact of the cross, though, has to lie in more than its graphic violence or its apparent unfairness. Many people have died cruel and unjust deaths. Many people have laid down their lives for good causes. Behind the image of the wood, nails, thorns and blood lays the mechanism of justice and mercy and that, for the artist who is a Christian, presents the ultimate challenge.

the times

Artists tend to be sensitive to the changing times, frequently so much so that they anticipate cultural shifts long before the general public. One of the valuable functions of art is its ability to deal with these shifts and prepare the population to look at the world in a new way.

This aspect of art can bother Christians because being responsive to the times can sound suspiciously like being shaped by the times. If we are not to be conformed to this world, doesn't that mean we should do our best to step outside of history? Don't timeless values suggest a timeless style of life? At its most extreme we can see this attitude in communities like the Hutterites and the Amish, where aspects of their lives are frozen in the seventeenth century because contact with the modern world is believed to corrupt.

The argument appears to be strengthened by the New Testament teaching that Christ is the "same yesterday and today and forever" (Hebrews 13:8). If Jesus doesn't change, shouldn't we follow his example? If the truth is unchanging, how can it be communicated through forms, such as art, which are subject to change?

But cultural change is inevitable. The days of David were not the same as the days of Noah; the days of Jesus were not the same as the days of Job. The human condition remains unchanged, but the way in which we discuss it and the priorities we give the details should take into account the way in which perceptions have changed. People once thought that our personalities were shaped by body fluids and that a clap of thunder was a sign of God's anger. In such a society words such as *blood, phlegm* and *lightning* would have had a completely different power than they hold for us today.

We may not trust every scientific discovery to be genuinely scientific, but there can be no doubt that today we know far more about how our bodies, our minds and the solar system work. These facts alone don't tell us anything about purpose or the origin of evil, but they help us understand who we are and why we behave the way we do. We no longer attribute all unusual human behavior to spirit possession because we know something about brain chemistry and psychological damage. We no longer consider solar eclipses, falling stars or bad weather omens because of our knowledge of meteorology and astronomy.

One of the effects of changing times is that people give priorities to different questions. This doesn't only happen from century to century but from decade to decade and even year to year. In the 1960s the issue of alienation was considered very important. It informed philosophy, painting, theater, poetry and music. Today the big questions are in the areas of sexuality, gender politics and the meaning of language itself. The word *alienation* is rarely heard when contemporary artists discuss the issues that preoccupy them.

If we are to enter the debate taking place in the contemporary art world, we have to listen to what is already being said before we contribute. This doesn't mean that if an issue hasn't been raised we can't say what we were going to say, but it may determine our timing and phraseology. This is a principle we use in normal social discourse. We listen to a group conversation and either comment on what is being said or wait for an opportunity to enter and raise something not already on the agenda.

Some years ago I was at an arts conference with a group of journalists discussing our work as Christians at national newspapers. On the last day someone arrived who had produced a newspaper for a drug charity. He came late, pulled up a chair and literally threw a bundle of his papers in the center of our circle. This is what a lot of Christians do in the art world: they don't listen to what has already been said; they don't sit for a while on the sidelines catching the drift of the arguments; they just assume that the world is waiting to hear what they have to say.

Each art form, and each genre within each art form, has its own conversation going on. If we want to be relevant we should discover the drift of the conversation, the talking points of today and the vocabulary being used. We should also listen to determine whether what we are most passionate about is on the agenda. If it is not, this may mean waiting patiently to establish yourself before making what might be interpreted as a controversial statement. Or it may mean subverting the art form, saying something that appears to mean one thing but that reveals another meaning later on.

Art responds to the times in a variety of ways. It responds in the first place to changes in technology, because new technology suggests new possibilities of combining art forms or of reaching new audiences. The art of the moving picture used the skills of the painter, photographer, actor, director and playwright, and eventually brought drama into almost every living room. There would be no rock music as we now know it without the discovery of electricity and the invention of the phonograph. Film animation has been transformed far more recently through digital technology.

Even within these art forms it is new technology that helps create the biggest developments. Think of the impact of adding sound to movies and then color. The success of the Beatles, great performing act that they were, can't be divorced from advances in studio recording, the development of stereo and the fact that teenagers owned their own record players and therefore were no longer dependent on their parents' approval as they would have been when there was one family gramophone in the living room.

New technology gives artists more to play with, but it can also involve a new way of looking at the world. The invention of photography in the nineteenth century not only provided the means for a new art form to develop but also affected the history of painting. Once it became possible for technology to reproduce scenes accurately, it released painters to approach reality in other ways and eventually led to experiments in perception such as impressionism and cubism. Photography raised new questions about what was real and how we perceive.

Christianity was profoundly affected by the invention of the printing press. It meant not only that the Bible became available to more people but that the Word of God was no longer something requiring ears and a good memory, but eyes and the ability to read and cross-reference. The ability to trace the development of ideas throughout the Bible is almost impossible without the written word, supplementary study guides and a concordance. There can be no doubt that those of us with Bibles see God in a different way than those relying on the spoken word.

Artists like to grapple with many of the same questions that concern philosophers and theologians, and so it is not surprising that new philosophical and theological ideas impact art. The postmodern theories of thinkers like Michel Foucault, Jean-François Lyotard, Roland Barthes, Jacques Derrida and Richard Rorty have affected many aspects of contemporary art, even in cases when the artists may not have read the source material.

The theories of religion and mythology promoted by the late Joseph Campbell have also had a huge impact, particularly on Hollywood screenwriters. Campbell, whose best known book is *The Hero with a Thousand Faces*,[1] believed that all the great myths and religious stories were variations on a single truth. His importance to film writers was that he suggested that the great myths were powerful because they corresponded to something true and permanent in the human condition, and that it was possible to identify the key elements and compose an archetypal journey. In other words, Hollywood could see the potential for making capital out of basic human spiritual yearning by marketing stories that drew on the tried and tested power of religion and myth.

One of Campbell's fans was story analyst Christopher Vogler, who was a consultant on such Disney films as *The Little Mermaid*, *Beauty and the Beast* and *The Lion King*. Vogler eventually wrote a book based on his insights titled *The Writer's Journey*, in which he described myth as "a special kind of story that deals with the gods or the forces of creation, and the relationship of these forces to human beings."[2]

Another fan was director George Lucas, who developed his idea for *Star Wars* after reading Campbell. He told Bill Moyers:

> I had to come up with a whole cosmology. . . . What do people believe in? I had to do something that was relevant, something that imitated a belief system that has been around for thousands of years and most people on this planet one way or another, have some kind of connection to.[3]

Theories of postmodernism and studies of mythology can be immensely stimulating to Christians. Although the conclusions of both are at variance with a Christian understanding, there is wisdom to be gleaned, and the ideas we end up disagreeing with can have the effect of making our faith more vital by forcing us to examine what we really believe. "As iron sharpeneth iron, so one man sharpens another" (Proverbs 27:17).

I think, for example, that Joseph Campbell was on to something. There is a surprising consistency in the pattern of myths. But whereas Campbell concludes that this proves they are all equally valid, I conclude that there is a template from which all grand narratives either develop or depart. In fact, I used the mythic structure suggested by Vogler's *The Writer's Journey* (itself based on Campbell's ideas) to help me make sense of Marvin Gaye's life when I came to write the biography *Trouble Man*, naming my chapters with titles taken from his stages of the journey.

Trends in science also affect art because artists are usually curious about new discoveries, and science throws up any number of "what if?" questions of the sort that artists like to play with. When a scientist conjectures that time could run backward, the novelist wants to write a story where all the action heads into the past. Predictions about computers with a greater intelligence than that of humans lead to movies about robots taking over the earth. It was, after all, a novelist, William Gibson, rather than a Silicon Valley specialist who coined the term *cyberspace*.[4]

Looking back we can see the effect of science on art. For instance, it's impossible to appreciate the writing of D. H. Lawrence without taking into account the then new theories about sexuality, religion and repression that were being published by Sigmund Freud. It is similarly impossible to fully understand the art of Salvador Dali without reference to both Freud and Jung and the significance they gave to the world of dreams.

Christians need have no fear of true science, although they do need to beware of the belief that science can solve all problems, material and spiritual, and can give us answers to the questions of "Why am I here?" "How should I behave?" and "Where am I going?" If science is a deeper understanding of what God has created—"thinking God's thoughts after him"—it can only increase reverence and worship.

For example, the discovery that the two hemispheres of the brain—right and left—apparently control different aspects of our personality can be useful in explaining behavior traits. It doesn't excuse sin and it doesn't relieve us of personal responsibility, but it can be a useful insight and can help us improve our creativity. However, other more dangerous ideas can intrude. I have sometimes seen it reported that our spirituality is controlled by a particular part of the brain, and it has been suggested that when people don't respond to religion it is because this part of their brain is underdeveloped. It has also been suggested that "spiritual experiences" could be induced by stimulating this area of the brain. This of course has to be rejected on the grounds that spiritual life doesn't reside in the brain and that spiritual life comes from God rather than from an electrical current.

Art receives influences from the places that artists travel to or the ethnic communities that artists are surrounded by. This is very obvious in rock music. In the 1950s it drew from the music of the black community and from the inheritors of folk tunes from England, Scotland and Ireland. In the 1960s it was considered unusual when the Beatles first introduced a sitar from India. In the 1970s a Caribbean influence was introduced, and now, as musicians travel the world freely and as ethnic groups in the big cities become more varied, there is a constant fusion of elements from Africa, America, Latin America, India and the Far East. As artists travel more widely they will inevitably draw inspiration from far more traditions. They will also be aware of the different role that art plays in cultures around the world.

This influence can worry Christians because they often equate cultural influences with religious influences. So to be influenced by Indian culture, they fear, is to be influenced by polytheism. Yet we have to remember that there are Christians in all countries, and the artists among them will express themselves in ways that draw from their own cultures. Rather than making these people more European or more American, we need to appreciate their art for the different ways in which it can help us see ourselves and God.

In a missionary newsletter I read a transcription of a spontaneous prayer given by a middle-aged Sudanese widow. I was struck with the fresh perceptions. She understood different things about God because of the poverty and famine she had endured. Her images were elemental, and her diction pulsed rather than flowed. How would we feel if someone stood up in our church and said, "I want to converse with you O God of the generations" or "I have grasped your hand, my God, my God. I have caught your hand. O God of the generations, I kiss your mouth. Discover me unawares in the place where I have been lost"?

A young American Christian, Paul-Gordon Chandler, wrote a book called *God's Global Mosaic*[5] in which he detailed the insights he had gathered from visiting Christians around the world. He said that from the Russians he learned about mystery and reverence. From Middle Eastern Christians he learned perseverance. The Latin American church taught him how to celebrate the gift of life. In India he came to reappraise the role of Jesus as a teacher. In Africa he found believers who had a deep experience of the freedom of God. In the Far East he was introduced to the idea that God can't be confined.

Art is also affected by political change. Even artists who don't make explicit political statements are affected by the ambiance. A time of financial instability can produce harsh realism that looks into the face of injustice and poverty (John Steinbeck) and light-hearted escapism that showcases dreams and fantasies (Fred Astaire). The Nazi extermination camps provided a new symbol for evil and also gave an immediacy to questions about the existence of a loving God and the nature of prejudice. During the Cold War period Western artists were very conscious of the potential for nuclear conflict, and this made apocalyptic themes more relevant.

Christians shouldn't create as if there is no ecological crisis, no famine, no abuses of human rights, no warfare, no genocide. If we're called to tend the earth, we should be concerned for its future. If we're called to love our neighbor, we should be concerned for their freedom and comfort. Sometimes we will get it wrong, fearing the collapse of the human race when it is only a bit of political indigestion, but it is better to respond than to think that political decisions are of no concern to God.

Being affected by the changes outlined above doesn't require conformity of response. Artists respond in a variety of ways. The development of new technology can tempt one artist to leave painting behind for computer graphics just as it might convince another artist to live as a hermit and paint icons. Fascism produced the Italian futurist poets, who sensed a bright new modern future, and a painter, the German George Grosz, who satirized the Nazis.

Christians often ignore the pressing questions of the day. This could be because they fear that even to understand the issues in depth might weaken their faith. Or it could be because they believe that timeless truths don't need to refer to contemporary anxieties. This is why the most common criticism of Christian art is that it is old-fashioned and irrelevant. In other words, it looks, sounds or reads like something from another period, and the issues it addresses are not the issues currently bothering people.

It can be disheartening to put the words *Christian* and *art* together in an Internet search engine. Instead of discovering something vital, perceptive, challenging and earth shaking, you are led to sites that display cute greetings cards, comforting verse and bland illustrations.

When I was researching my radio series *The History of Religion and Rock*[6] I taped songs by some leading CCM recording artists and gave them to the editor of a highly influential music paper to see what he would make of them. I then asked him what he thought. "I felt embarrassed," he told me. "The music is paralyzingly dated. There is no fire in it. There is no innovation and no energy. The music is basically a prop for the lyrics which sound like a groovy Californian sermon. The music and the words don't mesh together and the sentiments are pretty wet."[7]

Up-to-dateness, for its own sake, is not worth pursuing though. There is a lack of commitment and sincerity shown by artists who hijack trends to give the appearance of relevance. They inevitably get found out. They don't fully understand the genre because it didn't come naturally to them. It was borrowed from a subculture or a generation that they don't belong to.

The artists who ultimately gain respect have an imagination that is big enough to embrace trends but also, ultimately, to transcend them. For much of the 1960s Bob Dylan set the pace in rock music. He couldn't hope to maintain that position in the subsequent decades, and it would have been silly of him to try to adapt to punk, disco, grunge, rap or techno. What has sustained him is a commitment to his art; his best albums have always been ones in which he has clearly been sensitive to the changing times but has responded to them with an uncompromising musical vision.

Artists who are confident of their core vision are not afraid to produce something that might draw on past fashion, but they always do it knowingly. They know what they are doing, and their audience knows that they know. There is a huge difference between ironic references to the 1970s in the 1994 movie *Pulp Fiction* (directed by Quentin Tarantino) and an evangelistic film that mistakenly thinks that we are still living in the 1970s.

The Bible encourages us to know the times we live in and to choose our communication accordingly. In the final chapter of Ecclesiastes the writer explains how he has "searched to find just the right words" (Ecclesiastes 12:10). What a contrast to the attitude so often found among Christians of producing something unpolished and then praying for it to succeed. The writer of Ecclesiates was interested in fine-tuning. There were right words and wrong words. There were right words and almost right words. He had to weigh each word and consider what its effects would be. He knew that if he found what he was looking for they would pierce the consciousness and stay there like "firmly embedded nails" (Ecclesiastes 12:11). He wasn't interested in moving the emotions with a gentle tickle.

As we discussed in an earlier chapter, the choice of words and illustrations used by Jesus shows a concern for the mindset of his contemporaries. In one sense the stories of oil lamps, shepherds, lost coins, needle eyes and camels are harder for us to understand precisely because they were so tuned in to a particular stage of a particular culture. Jesus continually told his followers to be observant, to "watch and pray." It's no good praying if we don't also watch and no good watching if we don't also pray. The Pharisees and Sadducees were chided for having the ability to predict the weather but not being able to "interpret the signs of the times" (Matthew 16:3).

Although Paul's theology never wavers throughout his New Testament letters, he addresses each audience differently according to what he knows about them—he takes into account their culture. Is their background Jewish, Greek, Roman or pagan? He also takes into account their unique problems, questions and recent history. To each audience he brings something special from his own background as a Jew, Roman citizen, beneficiary of Greek culture and former Christ hater. The worldview doesn't change but the presentation does. The vocabulary is modified, the emphases vary, and the points are dealt with in greater or lesser detail.

Our best example of his communication strategy comes from the account of his visit to Athens in Acts 17. He spends time "reasoning" with both Jews and Greeks, inspects the idols on public display and then gives a talk, not in a religious center but in an arena well known for public debate. He goes to where the conversation on vital matters is already taking place. When he speaks he doesn't hold back with his core messaging, but his starting point is an affirmation of something good about them: they are religious. He then shows how he knows this. He has done his research. He has seen the altar inscribed "TO AN UNKNOWN GOD." Then he discusses general revelation, approvingly quoting their poet Aratus along the way, before leading his argument into the specifics of repentance, resurrection and judgment.

Acts 17 is clearly a summary of a long talk. It takes less than ninety seconds for us to read this summary, but Paul's argument may have gone on for hours just as his conversations with people in the marketplace went on "day by day." But the structure is presumably preserved and shows someone beginning with ideas familiar to his audience and gently building on those ideas.

I think that a good case could be made for Christians being even more able to anticipate cultural trends than our nonbelieving counterparts. We have the motivation to do so from the Bible. We have an incredible advantage in knowing the state of human nature and the facts of spiritual warfare. Then, to top it all, we have a conversational relationship with a God who knows what the future holds.

Of course God doesn't always share his secrets with us, but we can plead with him to prepare us now for the questions that are going to be asked in five, ten or even twenty years' time, and to prevent us from making art that gives the impression that the Creator and Sustainer of the universe can't keep up with the pace of modern life.

eight

the witness

I *s what I am calling for in this book possible? Can we imagine* Christians who are called to be artists rather than preachers, not only making an impact in their chosen form but doing so in a way that draws attention to a worldview that is different from that of their contemporaries, a worldview that gets people talking? Could it be that Christians will actually change the nature of the big debate?

Not only is it possible, but it is being done. I have chosen one example from the field of rock music partly because of my knowledge of music and partly because I know the individuals involved and have followed their story with particular interest. What they've done has embodied what I dreamed could be done when I heard "Woodstock" that afternoon in Switzerland.

When I started writing about music in 1970 I knew of no Christians operating at the highest level of rock, no one who was the equal of John Lennon, Jerry Garcia or Jim Morrison. I would hear rumors. Eric Clapton had come to the Lord. Keith Richards was a born-again believer. None of the rumors proved to be true.

Then things changed. In 1980 I was told of this "punk band from Dublin" where three of the four members were believers. Then I was given a tape of a session where singer Bono and guitarist the Edge had addressed a small group of Christian musicians telling them of their vision for rock music. It was quite extraordinary. Bono read from Isaiah 40:3: "In the desert prepare the way of the Lord, make straight in the wilderness a highway for our God." He felt that this verse summed up what they had been called to do.

Although any mistakes they have made over the past twenty years have been very public, U2 has expertly created a body of work which draws from the best traditions of modern music, adds something unique and incorporates a vision clearly rooted in the Bible. More than any other act in the history of rock, they have forced God, Jesus, the Bible and a Christian worldview on to the agenda. Rock critics could ignore the Jesus rock of the 1970s (and they did!), but they couldn't ignore U2; they had to voice an opinion about the values they stood for.

What U2 did worked because they had respect both for the form of rock 'n' roll and the content of Christianity. Their emerging view of the world was integrated into their art because they instinctively knew where timeless spiritual truths met youthful anxieties, ecstasies and idealisms. There had been many great rock songs about inarticulacy, but until "Gloria" (1981) there hadn't been one that extended the subject to include that feeling of not knowing what to pray, of the "groans that words cannot express" which Paul refers to in Romans. There had also been many songs about wanting to change the world but none that concluded with images from Matthew and Revelation until "New Year's Day" (1983).

In the early days of the band there was a zeal that indicated they felt they could only justify being in rock if a large number of specific statements were made in the lyrics. Behind the scenes there were those in their charismatic fellowship who suggested that the life of a rock star, which by its very nature was designed to attract attention, was at odds with the call of Christ to be humble servants. The band didn't dismiss this out of hand and were contemplating what God wanted them to do while writing songs for the album *October* (1981).

This explains the cries for guidance and the promise of submission in songs like "Gloria" and "Rejoice."

Even then Bono had the knack of writing lyrics as if with two minds, or perhaps it was with one mind contemplating two levels of reality. He could be writing about what he saw on television and then suddenly he was outside the tomb of Christ, or he could be writing about Polish workers and his mind drifted to the second coming. In "Surrender" on the *War* album (1983) he appeared to be writing about a girl on the street but then seemed distracted by some Pauline theology. " If I want to live," he writes, "I've got to die to myself someday."

These shifts have the effect of looking at one of those hologram cards. With ordinary perception we see the flat surface we call reality, but by turning the card we notice another dimension which was there all the time but not visible to us. Bono gazes at the commonplace but is soon transported into realms only the Christian can see, and then back again.

The three Christian members of U2 (Bono, Edge and drummer Larry Mullen) knew that there were dangers in rock 'n' roll but decided to live with the contradictions rather than give up. They also concluded that their existence wasn't justified by the amount of gospel they could dish out. The result was that they became less intense and Bono's faith flowed more naturally through his songwriting.

Looking back over a catalogue of ten albums from *Boy* (1980) to *All That You Can't Leave Behind* (2000) it's possible to place the songs using my model of the five concentric circles.

Some songs are exercises in sound or experiments with words. Bono uses a random phrase (for example, "Hawkmoon 269," "Unforgettable Fire," "Shadows and Tall Trees") as a springboard to an exercise in self-discovery. The words to "Is That All" were improvised in the studio after the musical ambiance had been created.

Producer Brian Eno in particular encouraged the band to pursue nonlinear methods of creation rather than turn prepared statements into songs. Sound checks and jam sessions were recorded so that new musical themes could be spotted. Mistakes, instead of being discarded, were used as clues to the existence of untapped ideas. One of Eno's mottoes was "Honor thy error as a hidden intention."

There is a second group of songs, more consciously constructed, which deal with shared human experiences. There are songs of love such as "With Or Without You," songs of death such as "One Tree Hill" and songs of doubt such as "The First Time." They don't always display an obvious Christian resolution because they don't need to. It's enough to share with an audience that, like them, you have loved, lost, celebrated and mourned.

Moving into the third circle there are the songs that show a biblically awakened conscience. Christ showed particular concern for the weak, poor, bereaved, alienated, exploited and marginalized, and it is right to expect to see that concern reflected in the art of his followers.

The effect of what U2 has said about personal faith in Christ would be considerably diminished if they hadn't been seen carrying out these commandments. I'm convinced that a lot of the respect that is now given to them has come because they are seen as men of their word. The gospel makes more sense to people when they can see it acted rather than only hear it spoken.

U2 has been in the forefront of rock music's involvement in global issues since 1985 when they appeared at Live Aid, a benefit concert for the people of Ethiopia. Besides Bono's personal visits to trouble spots and the band's collective involvement with organizations such as Amnesty International, Greenpeace and Jubilee 2000, U2 has released several powerful songs attempting to understand the plight of the world's bullied and broken.

"Silver and Gold" was a reflection on apartheid; "Red Hill Mining Town" entered the thoughts of a British mining community whose pits had been closed; "Mothers of the Disappeared" spoke on behalf of Argentineans who had lost their children during the reign of the military junta. Of course, any of these songs could have been written by a nonbeliever. But even though compassion is not exclusive to Christianity, it is essential, and U2 has been right to make these concerns such an integral part of their work.

Then we come to the second circle where we have songs that show a clear Christian distinctiveness but don't tie up all the loose ends. Sometimes, as was noted above, Bono uses a shifting perspective so that the attentive listener is introduced to something very earthly and then suddenly drawn into something altogether much bigger.

The song "Mysterious Ways," for example, begins with Johnny taking a walk. Johnny, from Chuck Berry onward, has been the rock 'n' roll everyman. In this song, however, his sister is the moon. This may remind us of St. Francis of Assisi and his prayer to "brother son and sister moon." Anyway, we know we're not dealing with Johnny B. Goode and that he's not looking for fulfillment in Hollywood. Then come the lines " If you want to kiss the sky/Better learn how to kneel." In "Purple Haze" Jimi Hendrix had the line "'scuse me while I kiss the sky," which was interpreted as a wild psychedelic fantasy. Could Bono be suggesting that for the ultimate transcendental experience you actually need to kneel in repentance and prayer?

Then comes the chorus of "She moves in mysterious ways," which appears to refer to the "sister moon," but the phrase "mysterious ways" is a reminder of the hymn lines written by the eighteenth-century Calvinist poet William Cowper: "God moves in a mysterious way/His wonders to perform." This allusion seems confirmed by the final chorus: "We move through miracle days/Spirit moves in mysterious ways."

In interviews Bono confirmed that the song had more than one level. "It's a song about women, or about woman," he said at one point. At another he said that the song related to his belief that "the spirit is a feminine thing." In the imagination of a Christian the seen points to the unseen.

At times Bono appears to soak himself in a particular chapter or book of the Bible and write a rock 'n' roll update. The track "40" is taken almost word for word from Psalm 40; "Fire" takes its imagery from Revelation; "With A Shout" revisits the Battle of Jericho; and "The Wanderer," sung by Johnny Cash (an appropriately world-weary believer) on the album *Zooropa* (1993), was Bono's five-minute version of Ecclesiastes and originally titled "The Preacher."

Not all the biblically inspired material is exhortation. One of the lessons Bono learned from the psalmists was that it was okay to debate with God. There are times when the Christian feels as down-hearted as anyone else, but instead of reaching for the trigger or the bottle he shouts at God, knowing that God has a habit of shouting back.

Sometimes these arguments appear to be in Bono's own voice—the Christian crying out for explanations—and at other times they appear to be in the voices of various disillusioned and hurt people. Songs like "If God Will Send His Angels" ("God has got his phone off the hook babe/Would he pick it up if he could?") and "mofo" ("Lookin' for to fill that God shaped hole") are like the psalms of the streets, the prayers of those who barely know how to pray.

"Drowning Man," a track on the album *War*, reverses the process. Instead of man calling out to God, God calls out to man, offering the hand of friendship. The most compelling attraction of Christianity to Bono as a teenager was the idea that God was interested in him. Not a god, but God. "What are we told to base this relationship on?" he asked. "The relationship is to begin with the Father, then Christ, who is the Son of the Father."[1]

What stands the test of eternity is a theme that runs through *All That You Can't Leave Behind*. What gets left behind when we die, and what are we able to take with us? The album cover shows the four members of the group standing in an airport and evokes those feel-ings that we have when we fly and entertain the thought, however fleetingly, of what would happen should this be our final flight. The image printed on the CD is a woman and child, seen from a distance on the cover, blurred and reminiscent of cinematic images of near-death experiences, of people headed toward an unknown future.

The song from which the title is taken, "Walk On," appears to refer to 1 Corinthians 13 and the teaching that of all the gifts we have only love will survive beyond death.

> The only baggage you can bring
> Is all that you can't leave behind.

On the same album the song "Grace" is about what the title suggests—a "thought that changed the world," as the lyric refers to it. Bono pictures grace as something feminine which makes "beauty out of ugly things."

> Grace, she takes the blame
> She covers the shame
> Removes the stain
> It could be her name.

This brings us to the circle at the center. How does a rock band deal with the deeply unfashionable subject of the cross? It seems that U2, because of the excitement of their music and the strength of their vision, was able to achieve things that weaker, less imaginative artists would never have been able to.

"Sunday Bloody Sunday" (the title refers to the killing of Irish marchers by British troops in 1972) moves from some general musing on violent conflict to the causes ("the trenches dug within our hearts") to the ultimate solution ("The real battle just begun/To claim the victory Jesus won/On a Sunday, bloody Sunday"). Thus the blood has become the blood of Christ and the Sunday has become Easter Day.

"Pride (In the Name of Love)" ends up being about the assassination of Martin Luther King Jr., but the preamble is about Christ. Who else do we know who came in the name of love, who came to justify, who resisted violence and who was betrayed with a kiss? The link with King illustrates the continuity of peaceful revolution and the powerful shadow that Christ's sacrifice has cast over history.

As the group's writing has matured, the approaches have become more subtle. "Until the End of the World," which can seem to be set in a gay bar if you're not paying attention, is actually set in Gethsemane. It's a song written in the voice of Judas Iscariot sometime between his action of betrayal and his suicide. "When Love Comes to Town," an experiment in blues, begins conventionally enough, but by the end we realize that the love that is coming (or has come) is the love of Christ. The narrator of the final verse is a Roman soldier who gambled for Christ's clothing and who has "seen love conquer the great divide."

"I Still Haven't Found What I'm Looking For" was a deliberate antidote to the kind of smug art that implies that everything in our lives can be sorted out after a quick prayer of faith. We live between two great events—the cross and the coming of the kingdom—and as such, live in tension. We're not as messed up as we were but we're not as sorted out as we will be. About what Christ has already accomplished the song is uncompromising:

> You broke the bonds, loosed the chains,
> carried the cross, of my shame
> You know I believe it.

About what he will one day accomplish the song is equally clear:

> I believe in the Kingdom Come
> Then all the colors will bleed into one.

But at the same time, Bono is aware of contradictions and compromises. He can speak with the tongue of an angel but can still reach out for the hand of the devil. He's reached the mountaintop, but he's still running.

> People expect you, as a believer, to have all the answers, when really
> all you have is a new set of questions. . . . I think that if "I Still Haven't

Found What I'm Looking For" is successful, it's because it's not affirmative in the ordinary way of a gospel song. It's restless, yet there is a pure joy in there somewhere.[2]

U2's influence has been considerable. They have affected not only the development of rock music but have been a significant force in the recent renaissance of Irish culture. Bono's personal power, unusual for a rock star, extends well beyond the boundaries of rock music. When the twenty-year-old convert told of his vision back in 1980, could he have dreamed that he would be asked to write the introduction to a paperback volume of Psalms, that he would be called in to persuade the pope to play a part in reducing third-world debt or that he would see in the new century in the company of the president of the United States?

The band's original vision was to make ready a path for the Lord, and I think they have done that by putting issues close to the heart of the Christian faith on the agenda. They have not only supplied a role model for Christian musicians who didn't want to enter the CCM market, but they have made it acceptable for anyone within rock to ruminate about God, Jesus and redemption.

They have also carried out their business in a way that is consistent with their ethical concerns. The royalties are split equally four ways regardless of who wrote the songs, they employ far more women than most rock bands, and they have resisted leaving their hometown and moving to Los Angeles or London because they believe it was important to stay close to their roots. The effect of the band remaining in Dublin, once considered an outback as far as rock music was concerned, has been to increase local pride and put Ireland firmly on the entertainment map.

Exactly thirty years from my visit to L'Abri in Switzerland things have changed in rock music. Among the cacophony of voices there is a Christian contribution. Theirs is by no means the only way of doing it, but it is one way of doing it, and they have achieved it by "remaining in the situation which they were in when God called them" (1 Corinthians 7:20, my paraphrase).

I hear of similar movements in other art forms where artists have comfortably integrated a faith-inspired vision and are respected by their peers. Hollywood screenwriter Randall Wallace *(Braveheart, The Man in the Iron Mask)* majored in religion at Duke University and then spent a year at Duke Divinity School before becoming a writer. Even critics unaware of his background have noted the spiritual principles and biblical allusions evident in his work. Wallace credits his desire to tell stories with his early exposure to revivalist preaching and the Bible. *"Braveheart* is a pure sermon that I could preach from any pulpit, but more people would get the message if it were a film," he said. "It's about whether integrity costs something and what it takes to pay the price."[3]

One of Australia's most talented contemporary fiction writers is Tom Winton, who says that he has spent "a lifetime journeying in a religious faith against the current in the least religious country in the world."[4] His work is undeniably shaped as much by the Pentecostalism of his early years as it is by his present-day Anglicanism. In novels like *Cloudstreet* and *That Eye, The Sky* he creates a world where spiritual manifestations appear perfectly natural in the ordinary, slightly run-down world. They are the work of someone who, as a child, felt that he experienced God as much through landscape, art and literature as he did through the activities of church. "Right from the start a good part of the sustenance I had in my faith was through the signals that God's world was sending me," he says. "Yet, in the religious tradition I grew up in, that could never be admitted or discussed."[5]

Sometimes the work of these Christians is distinguished not by overt statements but by an innate goodness that people recognize. It is clearly the talent of some people to create works that embody love, joy, peace, kindness and gentleness rather than expound on them. The British animator Nick Park, creator of such films as *Creature Comforts* (1990), *The Wrong Trousers* (1993) and *Chicken Run* (2000), has developed characters which exude a heartwarming blend of decency and eccentricity. He recognizes that his stories are driven by personal observations of human behavior rather than by a grand message. "I don't want to have an agenda," he says. "I think my faith does come through, so in that sense I suppose there is an agenda, but it is quite a subtle one. You've got to respect your audience and not try to do their thinking for them."[6]

This attitude is echoed by another animator, Pete Docter, a writer and supervising animator on the *Toy Story* films, who says that he feels uncomfortable with the idea of expressly building a film around a moral. "If you actually come out and say it, it loses its power." He believes that art is essentially about expressing those things which can't be captured in language. "You can say it in words, but it's always just beyond the reach of actual words, and you're doing whatever you can to communicate a sense of something that is beyond you."[7]

I'm sure that the faith of people like Park and Docter affects their work in more profound ways than they are perhaps aware. This is how *Toy Story 2* (1999) affected Christopher Tookey, the film critic of London's *Daily Mail* newspaper:

> Woody is well adjusted enough to make the right decisions—in favour of having a personal life, with genuine friends and sincere relationships, but also the certainty of growing old and of being outgrown. In short, Woody picks humanity and mortality. And, of course, the story of Woody has a religious significance. For Christians believe that Jesus, too, turned his back on immortality and chose to live and die as a human. *Toy Story 2* wears its religious themes lightly. But its positive, uplifting message—in favour of love, commitment and responsibility—comes across loud and clear.[8]

Each of them, in their own way, is helping to shape the nature of the debate in our culture. They are putting things of importance back on the agenda and it becomes more difficult to ridicule or ignore the concerns of Christianity when respected artists are dealing with them imaginatively. The best art doesn't tell people what to believe but enables them, for a short while, to see things differently, and the Christian can enable people to momentarily glimpse the world through eyes that have been touched by Christ.

> So I try to be like you
> Try to feel it like you do
> But without you it's no use. ("When I Look At The World," U2)

the life

Why aren't there more Christians involved at the heart of the arts scene? This book has dealt with some of the theological misunderstandings that might either have deterred Christians from becoming artists or have made it difficult for them to effectively express their renewed view of the world.

Something I haven't yet touched on is the spiritual life of the artist. Over the years I have seen many people get close to a position where they seemed poised to create a little divine disturbance, and then they have been destroyed by the very values they set out to challenge.

My first experience was with a friend, Dave, a poet and a singer. Dave's shelves were cluttered with rock biographies, Beat poetry and Puritan commentaries. He had a great ability, it seemed, to negotiate his way between the worlds of Reformed theology and bohemian subculture.

Many of us thought that Dave would be the first artist to get up there with Mick Jagger, John Lennon and Van Morrison, and add a Christian strand to the discussion. His lyrics were startlingly sensuous, and yet all the way through his songs was a strong biblical understanding. We thought he was on the brink of great things when the former manager of the singer Donovan took an interest in his career and Mick Taylor, then the Rolling Stones lead guitarist, played on some of his demo recordings.

But Dave's career didn't take off due to the usual music business disappointments. He borrowed money and ran out of money. Some time in the mid-1970s, he became involved with a Jesus people-type commune. This was most unlike him although understandable in some ways because he was always driven to extremes.

Dave now became overtly "spiritual." He preached and led Bible studies. He reformed his band and they played Jesus rock. Knowing his talents as I did, I wondered whether this was the best use of them. But for the first time in his life he was comfortably settled, had a recording contract and was playing regular concerts.

His ardor soon cooled, though, and he became more interested in the tape manufacturing plant he had set up to duplicate Christian tapes. He became a businessman. He stopped going to church. He began to manage other bands. Then he spent almost all his time away from his wife and family. Drugs entered the picture. Then other women. The last time I saw him I took the unusual step (for me) of inquiring after his spiritual health. "All I know," he said, "is that God loves me."

I was in America in 1980 when a call came through informing me that Dave had been killed in a car accident. He'd run into the back of a truck which had jackknifed on a highway in the early hours of the morning. An autopsy found cocaine in his blood. At his funeral several people stood in front of his coffin and spoke of his faith, but as I walked from the crematorium behind two of his more recent musical acquaintances, one said to the other, "I never knew that he was religious."

Although no one else I know has followed a trajectory exactly like my friend, I have known many who have started out with a vision to be a voice that counts in the arts world and have ended up being victims of the culture they set out to transform. In almost all of the cases the change hasn't been sudden but has taken the form of a gradual compromise until, eventually, their hearts went cold toward God.

The problem starts when we don't take the idea of spiritual warfare seriously. Where influence is concentrated the devil will be most active because his power is limited, and therefore he needs to focus his efforts at strategic points. Fortunately for us we're not given details of how these battles are fought, only that there are "powers of this dark world" and "spiritual forces of evil in the heavenly realms" against which we need to protect ourselves with "the full armor of God" (Ephesians 6:12, 13).

I'm convinced that the world of the arts, media and entertainment, because of its access to the imaginations of so many millions, is a place of great interest to the spiritual forces of evil. As a movie director recently observed, "L.A. is the town that controls world storytelling for both children and adults." You only have to read a book like Peter Biskind's *Easy Riders, Raging Bulls: The Story of Hollywood in the 1970s*[1] to see how so much talent is destroyed by decadence.

Artists have no special protection. In fact, because of their tendency to be curious about all forms of experience and their need to avoid rigid forms of thinking, they are probably more vulnerable to temptation. The standard protection kit offered to all Christians is the belt of truth, the breastplate of righteousness, the shoes of readiness, the shield of faith, the helmet of salvation, the sword of the Spirit and prayer (Ephesians 6). We can't survive with the T-shirt of Sunday school memories and the baseball cap of personal vision.

Our motives for wanting to be in the art world need to be examined. The arts can do wonders for the ego and therefore attract those whose major motivation is to be known and recognized. The history of rock music is littered with people who wanted fame as a form of revenge against those who made them feel unwanted when they were children.

Wanting to be an artist in the service of God sounds like the purest of motives, but it can be corrupted. What if we're privately imagining that such a promise to serve God might put us in the fast track or that if we can catch God's view of reality we will be heralded as visionaries? What if our hidden motive is that we want to be revered by the Christian community and mark ourselves off from the ordinary person in the pew? The actress Tallulah Bankhead was asked why she got into the theater and she replied, "To get out of the audience." Some of us can get into the arts in order to get out of the congregation.

When we start to get work accepted by galleries, theaters, publishers or film studios we naturally feel elated. There is an honorable satisfaction that comes from seeing your name on the spine of a book or in the credits at the end of a movie. But we have to be on form to discern between the satisfied pride in a job well done and the pride that puffs up or precedes a fall.

We easily fall into the temptation of thinking of ourselves as better than others or at least thinking that our understanding of the world is sharper. Temperamentally, artists often relish being outsiders who look in at society but who are not really a part of it. Some believe that their perceptions are only kept sharp by disengaging themselves. When a Christian songwriter friend of mine, noted for his bizarre behavior, was asked why he couldn't act like normal people he replied, "If I acted like a normal person I would start to see the world like a normal person and I would no longer write songs."

This desire to be an outsider fits in well with the Christian idea of being in but not of the world, of being a pilgrim and a sojourner. The prophets, Jesus and Paul were all wanderers whose views clashed with those of the majority and who faced the hostility of the ruling class. None of them put any store by possessions or status, and they loved to sit around and debate the big issues. The Bible seems full of role models for would-be bohemians.

When it comes to church there is an obvious conflict for the constitutional outsider who doesn't like belonging to organizations, hates the routine of having to be in the same place at the same time every week and finds it hard to fraternize with people who "don't understand." Yet lack of fellowship with a recognized body of Christians is the most common cause of artists loosening the moorings of their faith and then eventually becoming ineffective.

I speak from experience. When I first came to London I attended a good church, but then I began to think that the sermons weren't really addressing the issues that preoccupied me. To do that, I read books of theology. Pretty soon the reading of theology had replaced the church, and I was becoming what some people would call a Lone Ranger Christian.

I was making myself a special case. The majority of Christians needed the structure of church, but as an artist, I didn't. I had nothing in common with ordinary churchgoers; they weren't my kind of people. The standards of presentation I expected were so much higher than the church's. Things presented as art—sketches and songs, for example—offended me because they weren't professional.

I wasn't alone. I knew many musicians, painters, poets, dancers and actors who felt uncomfortable in church. I had friends who thought that having a meal with a couple of Christians constituted fellowship and others who worshiped in the church of their own hearts. In many cases churches had failed to inspire and nurture these people. In other cases I'm sure that they had developed a false sense of self-importance and were being kept back by pride.

The writer Kathleen Norris had been on the fringes of the Warhol crowd in the New York of the 1970s. Then she returned to her family roots in the Dakotas and also to the faith she first encountered as a child. Her experience of attending small rural churches after years in the big-city art scene will sound familiar to many: "I wasn't prepared for the pain," she wrote in *Dakota: A Spiritual Geography.* "The services felt like word bombardment—agony for a poet—and often exhausted me so much I'd have to sleep for three or more hours afterward. Doctrinal language slammed many a door in my face, and I became frustrated when I couldn't glimpse the Word behind the words."[2]

Jack Clemo was a celebrated British poet and also a Calvinistic Methodist. Blind and deaf from an early age, Clemo at one time drifted away from the Methodism of his youth and began to find spiritual solace in nature. He didn't feel that the village Methodists understood the way he saw life, and he felt isolated. In 1949 he wrote, "I felt that perhaps we did not need the church any more, but only the church dogmas divorced from their ecclesiastical setting and rendered elemental by faith."[3]

Later in his life he returned to the church. In 1977 he explained the change:

> At first I steered clear of the church, having a sort of "poetry religion," but a Christian can't develop much on "poetry religion." We all need the religion of ordinary people and the love of other converts. That's why, in the end, I went back to church; to worship around people who don't like poetry. It's a good discipline. I can't put myself apart from them as someone very special. As a convert I am just an ordinary believer, worshipping the same Lord as they do.[4]

The church humbles us. It is one of the few places in our societies today where we sit with rich and poor, young and old, black and white, educated and uneducated, and are focused on the same object. It is one of the few places where we share the problems and hopes of our lives with people we may not know. It is one of the few places where we sing as a crowd. Although the church needs its outsiders to prevent it from drifting into dull conformity, the outsiders need the church to stop them from drifting into individualized religion.

Church life can be hard for the celebrity artist. They may not consider themselves to be special but everyone else does, and this makes it impossible to worship in the normal way. How can they share in a fellowship group when their problems can be quickly translated into newspaper headlines? How can they build up friendships when everyone is trying to slip them a demo tape or a screenplay?

Unfortunately, this means that the higher the public profile, the less likely someone is to have a normal church life. The less church life they have, the more prone they are to developing idiosyncratic theologies and leading lives that are not subject to the scrutiny of more mature Christians or accountable to elders. At the very moment when they need to be tanking up on teaching and preaching and grounding themselves in fellowship they are cut free from both the doctrine and the community. At the point that they are required to give out the most they are taking in the least.

Two things were particularly helpful to me during my time of struggle. The first was the formation of an organization to help Christians involved in the arts—the Arts Centre Group in London—where we met on a regular basis to talk through issues that were unique to our combination of work and faith. Here we were able not only to debate theology and art theory but to meet Christians across the disciplines. It would have been difficult for me to meet Christian dancers, painters, photographers, filmmakers, poets, novelists, graphic designers, actors and architects through normal church circles. At the ACG I would meet such people regularly and a lot of cross-fertilization took place—filmmakers working with poets, illustrators working with authors, songwriters working with painters.

An ordinary church often doesn't have the experience to deal with the special issues facing artists. Some congregations might feel it's wrong for a singer to entertain in a bar, so how could they possibly offer advice on the more complex problems of art and behavior?

The second helpful move for me was to share an apartment with fellow Christians. In my case, at different times, I shared with a filmmaker, four architects and a creator of radio commercials. We had regular prayer times to keep us on track, were there to offer each other comfort or advice and had discussions about Christianity and art in the kitchen, on the staircase, over meals and even through the bathroom door.

We met each other's friends, lived through each other's dilemmas and supported each other's work. If I think back and try to work out where I reached certain conclusions about faith and art, the answer inevitably is that it was in that apartment, during a routine conversation. Whatever we did we knew that we would have to justify it to each other.

If the quality of the Christian's spiritual life suffers, then he or she will never be able to compete with the best that the world can offer. Nonbelievers don't have an objective value system to live up to. They may have ideals, but these can be constantly adapted to the times. They can allow themselves to be dictated by their fallen nature. But for the Christian there is the tussle between the old nature and new nature.

A lot of our art making is instinctive. What compels us to create is something inside that needs to get out. That is why the quality of our interior life is so important. If we are living righteously and God's laws are constantly before us, then the imaginations of our heart will reflect that. If we are constantly learning from Scripture, even our unconscious will be being purified, and our dreams will be different from the dreams of the unregenerate person.

It's only when our thoughts and our behavior are brought in line with God's will that we can fulfill T. S. Eliot's hope of an art that is "unconsciously Christian." If we care little about Christian obedience and then endeavor to create art that reflects a Christian perspective, then we have lost our integrity (defined by the *Concise Oxford Dictionary* as "the state of being whole. The condition of being unified or sound in construction"). We are acting a role.

I have found that some of my clearest and most apparently "spiritual" writing has come when I've abandoned the big task of trying to say something profound and am just fooling around with words. This is because I then unconsciously draw on the reserves accumulated over years of knowing God. I'm more likely to come up with great insights while writing about a coffee mug or a cereal packet than if I contemplate *la condition humaine.*

I think this is what Bono was getting at when he talked about the U2 track "Where the Streets Have No Name," which started off as a phrase from his experience of Ethiopian refugee camps and ended up being about wanderlust and heaven. "It has one of the most banal couplets in the history of pop music, " he said, "but it also contains some of the biggest ideas. In a curious way, that seems to work. If you get too heavy about these things, you don't communicate. But if you're flip or throwaway about it, then you do. That's one of the paradoxes I've had to come to terms with."[5]

I know that it is what the poet Luci Shaw meant when she examined her poem "Saved by Optics," about an experiment to create fire by using a lens of ice, and found reflections of faith: "I had felt no compelling theological motivation to write this poem," she said, "simply a fascination with an intriguing physical phenomenon. But much later, as I reread the completed poem with a more critical eye . . . I became aware of some correspondences that had until then escaped my attention."[6]

We can probably all think of examples of people whose lives became corrupted but who continued to put forward Christian truths in their work. There is the gospel singer who cheated on his wife, the filmmaker who was caught up in a web of "financial irregularities," the writer who cynically churned out what he knew the market wanted while indulging in secret vices.

Young missionary Jim Elliot, famed for his death in 1956 at the hands of the Auca Indians he was attempting to reach, wrote in his diary in February 1950:

> I see tonight that in spiritual work, if nowhere else, the character of the worker decides the quality of the work. Shelley and Byron may be moral free-lancers and still write good poetry. Wagner may be lecherous as a man, and still produce fine music, but it cannot be so in any work for God.
>
> Paul could refer to his own character and manner of living for proof of what he was saying to the Thessalonians. Nine times over in the first epistle he says, "You know," referring to the Thessalonians' first-hand observation of Paul's private as well as public life. Paul went to Salonica and lived a life that more than illustrated what he preached; it went

beyond illustration to convincing proof. No wonder so much work in the Kingdom today is shoddy—look at the moral character of the worker.[7]

People who are Christians can still succeed in the arts while living sub-Christian lives. But the witness will eventually disappear from their work. They won't be contributing to the big debate. They will begin to remain silent about controversial issues because they no longer want to risk being persecuted. Fame, money and critical respect have a subtle way of cooling spiritual ardor.

In 1994 I interviewed a musician in New York who had been very open about his Christian faith in the secular press. He told me about his conversion through reading the Gospels at the age of twenty-three and the help given him by a youth pastor. Typically for an artist he was not attracted to the institutional aspects of Christianity but to the dynamism of Christ.

I was excited that someone who was so successful in his particular genre of music was so unapologetic about his beliefs. But I was also aware of those signs that often herald a weakening. He was cautious about calling himself a Christian, preferring the description "lover of Christ." He was also out of fellowship. "I haven't found a church, but I've been looking," he said, going on to say that he wanted something "like the way the apostles met. Just a few people getting together."

In 2000 I saw him quoted in one magazine as saying "I don't really call myself a Christian in a traditional sense, nor do I feel connected to any specific religious dogma." In another source he said, "Indulgence can lead to epiphanies more times than abstinence. Getting drunk and having inappropriate sex with someone, you learn about yourself. It thrusts you into the commonality of things."

Instead of resisting the predominant view he bought into it. I think his mistake came when he disassociated himself from the church. It sounds wonderfully pure to declare that you are a "lover of Jesus," but if you truly love Jesus you will love his church (including that part of it now in heaven) and his teachings.

My original title for this book was, as I have already mentioned, *Being There*. This was, of course, suggested by the Jerzy Kosinski novel and the later film starring Peter Sellers. I chose it because, reduced to a single phrase, that was what I felt I was calling Christians in the arts to do. I was calling them not to a particular strategy and definitely not to a special subculture, but to simply "be there" where it counts and create something different and challenging by staying faithful and allowing that faith to invade their vision.

I was privileged to know the British journalist Malcolm Muggeridge. He was an early role model for me in my journalism because he had a wide knowledge of the world picked up over years working as a foreign correspondent, broadcaster and magazine editor, but he had also developed an acute spiritual insight after a conversion fairly late in life.

One day when talking to him at his home in the Sussex countryside I asked him what a Christian in the arts or media should be doing today. I thought that because of his well-known iconoclasm and love of satire he would suggest some clever way in which we could topple the false gods of our society. I waited to hear his plan. But what he said surprised me, because he was more concerned with our personal faithfulness than our grand plans.

> I think really, that as in all other fields, we must be Christian. That is essentially what a Christian has to do. There are some Christians who I have met in the media and their influence has been out of proportion to what it might seem to be, just because they were Christians and were known to be Christians. I don't think that a Christian has to be a particular type of Christian to be a diplomat, or a particular sort of Christian to be a doctor, or a particular sort of Christian to be a laborer. He has, in all circumstances, to be a Christian.

If we want to see art that challenges the prevailing secularism we need artists who are not only skillful but also theologically well equipped, grounded in a fellowship and living obedient lives.

Christianity is not a mere philosophy, it is a spiritual relationship that results in changed thoughts and actions, and it will only rub off on our work if it has first of all permeated our lives. As the late political activist Jerry Rubin once wrote, "Revolution is only as high as the people that make it."[8]

Notes

Chapter 1: The Vision

[1]Timothy Leary, *The Politics of Ecstasy* (London: Paladin, 1970).

[2]Garrison Keillor, *Lake Wobegon Days* (New York: Viking Penguin, 1985).

[3]J. Marks, *Rock and Other Four Letter Words* (New York: Bantam, 1968).

[4]Calvin Tomkins, *Ahead of the Game* (London: Penguin, 1968).

[5]John Russell Taylor, *Anger and After* (London: Methuen, 1962).

[6]Francis Schaeffer, *The God Who Is There* (Downers Grove, Ill.: InterVarsity Press, 1968).

[7]Harry Blamires, *The Christian Mind* (New York: Seabury Press, 1963).

[8]T. S. Eliot, *Selected Essays* (London: Faber & Faber, 1932).

[9]Robert Short, *The Gospel According to Peanuts* (Richmond, Va.: John Knox Press, 1965).

[10]Max Roach, in Ted Gioia, *The History of Jazz* (New York: Oxford University Press, 1997).

Chapter 2: The Church

[1]Owen Chadwick, *A History of Christianity* (New York: St. Martin's Press, 1995).

[2]G. B. Harrison, *Introducing Shakespeare* (London: Penguin, 1939).

[3]Andries Pels, in *The Oxford Dictionary of Art*, ed. Ian Chilvers (London: Oxford University Press, 1997).

[4]William Wilberforce, in Reginald Coupland, *Wilberforce* (London: Collins, 1923).

[5]George Müller, in Roger Steer, *George Müller: Delighted in God* (London: Hodder & Stoughton, 1975).

[6]Daniel Defoe, *Robinson Crusoe* (London, 1719).

[7]Ian Watt, *The Rise of the English Novel* (London: Chatto & Windus, 1957).

[8]John Ritchie, in Neil Dickson, "The Brethren and Literature," *Aware*, June 1991.

[9]David A. Noebel, *Rhythms, Riots and Revolution* (Tulsa, Okla.: Christian Crusade, 1966).

[10]David A. Noebel, *Communism, Hypnotism and the Beatles* (Tulsa, Okla.: Christian Crusade, 1964).

[11]Coleman, Dowell, in "An Interview with Coleman Dowell," by John O'Brien, *Review of Contemporary Fiction* 2, no. 2 (1982).

[12]John Henry Newman, *Essays Critical and Historical*, vol. 2, in H. S. Bowden, *The Religion of Shakespeare* (London: Burns & Oates, 1899).

[13]Martin Scorcese, in *Scorcese on Scorcese*, ed. David Thompson and Ian Christie (London: Faber & Faber, 1989).

[14]Flannery O'Connor, *Mystery and Manners* (New York: Farrar Strauss Giroux, 1961).

Chapter 3: The World

[1]Thomas Watson, *The Ten Commandments* (Edinburgh: Banner of Truth, 1965).

[2]Peter Fuller, *Images of God* (London: Hogarth, 1990).

[3]Billy Sunday, in Lee Thomas, *Billy Sunday* (Van Nuys, Calif.: Bible Voice, 1975).

[4]Daniel Defoe, *Moll Flanders* (London, 1722).

[5]François Mauriac, interview by Jean le Marchand, in *Writers at Work*, ed. Malcolm Cowley (New York: Viking, 1958).

[6]T. S. Eliot, *Selected Essays* (London: Faber & Faber, 1932).

[7]Richard Lovelace, *Dynamics of Spiritual Life* (Downers Grove, Ill.: InterVarsity Press, 1979), p. 93.

[8]Thomas Howard, *Christ the Tiger* (New York: J. B. Lippincott, 1967).

[9]Bruno Bettelheim, *The Uses of Enchantment* (New York: Alfred A. Knopf, 1976).

[10]Steve Turner, *Trouble Man: The Life and Death of Marvin Gaye* (New York: Ecco/HarperCollins, 2000).

Chapter 4: The Split

[1]Arthur Miller, introduction to *Arthur Miller Plays: One* (London: Methuen, 1988).

[2]Don Patterson, "The Dilemma of the Peot [sic]," in *How Poets Work*, ed. Tony Curtis (Brigend, U.K.: Seren, 1996).

[3]W. B. Yeats, "Essay."

[4]"Turn Your Eyes upon Jesus" (Helen Lemmel).

[5]Flannery O'Connor, *Mystery and Manners* (New York: Farrar Strauss Giroux, 1961).

[6]Plato *Phaedo* 66-67, in Steve Shaw, *No Splits* (London: Marshall Pickering, 1989).

Chapter 5: The Bible

[1]Leo Tolstoy, *What Is Art?* (London: Oxford University Press, 1950).

[3]Matthew Fox, *Original Blessing: A Primer in Creation Spirituality* (Santa Fe, N.M.: Bear, 1983).

[4]Bono, introduction to *Psalms* (Edinburgh: Canongate, 1999).

[5]Samuel Beckett, *Waiting for Godot* (London: Faber & Faber, 1956).

[6]J. D. Salinger, *The Catcher in the Rye* (Boston: Little, Brown, 1951).

[7]Robert Jamieson, A. R. Fausset, and David Brown, *Commentary on the Whole Bible*, rev. ed. (Grand Rapids, Mich.: Zondervan, 1961).

[8]Bill Mallonee, "Love Cocoon," *Slow Dark Train*, Vigilantes of Love, Capricorn Records, 1997.

[9]Ezra Pound, *ABC of Reading* (London: Routledge, 1934).

[10]Robert Lowth, *Lectures on the Sacred Poetry of the Hebrews* (London, 1787).

[11]R. G. Collingwood, *Essays in the Philosophy of Art* (Bloomington: Indiana University Press, 1964).

Chapter 6: The Mind

[1]Harry Blamires, *The Christian Mind* (New York: Seabury, 1963).

[2]"I Am His and He Is Mine" (George Wade Robinson).

[3]Blamires, *Christian Mind*.

[4]Owen Chadwick, *A History of Christianity* (New York: St. Martin's Press, 1995).

[5]Gerard Manley Hopkins, "God's Grandeur," in *The Poems of Gerard Manley Hopkins*, ed. Robert Bridges (London: Oxford University Press, 1937).

[6]Louis Vauxcelles, in George Rouault, *Bernard Dorival* (Naefels, Switzerland: Bonfini, 1984).

[7]Jeremy Seabrook, *Unemployment* (London: Quartet, 1982).

[8]William Golding, *Lord of the Flies* (London: Faber & Faber, 1954).

[9]Anthony Burgess, *A Clockwork Orange* (London: Heinemann, 1962).

[10]J. R. R. Tolkien, *Tree and Leaf* (London: Allen & Unwin, 1964).